# Contents

# Notes on contributors

**Professor Peter Beresford OBE** has a long-standing involvement in issues of participation as a researcher, activist, educator and writer. He is Professor of Social Policy and Director of the Centre for Citizen Participation at Brunel University and Chair of Shaping Our Lives, the national disabled people's and service users' organisation and network. He is author of *A straight talking guide to being a mental health service user* (PCCS Books, 2007).

**Dr Kathy Boxall** is a psychiatric system survivor. Kathy previously wrote about her experiences of being a mental health service user using the pseudonym 'Anne Wilson'. She now works as a Lecturer in the Department of Sociological Studies, University of Sheffield, and writes under her own name.

**Dr Sarah Carr** is a Senior Research Analyst at the Social Care Institute for Excellence (SCIE), a Visiting Fellow of the Centre for Government and Charity Management, London South Bank University, and a Fellow of the Royal Society of Arts. She is an editor of *Disability and Society*. As well as being on the board of the National Survivor and User Network (NSUN), Sarah is a trustee of the LGB&T Consortium of Voluntary and Community Organisations. She is a long-term user of mental health services and was a member of the NICE Guideline Development Group for 'Service user experience of adult mental health: improving the experience of care for people using adult NHS mental health services'. Sarah has written on her own experiences as well as: mental health practice and policy; LGB welfare and equality issues; the personalisation agenda in social care and health; and service user participation.

**David Evans** is Professor in Health Services Research (Public Involvement) in the Faculty of Health and Life Sciences, University of the West of England (UWE), Bristol (http://people.uwe. ac.uk/Pages/person.aspx?accountname=campus\dh-evans). His research interests focus on public involvement in health, including involvement in research. He is currently leading a National Institute for Health (NIHR) funded research project assessing the impact of public involvement in research through a realist evaluation. David is also a member of the NIHR INVOLVE Advisory Group. He takes a lead on public involvement in research for his UWE faculty

# MENTAL HEALTH SERVICE USERS IN RESEARCH

## Critical sociological perspectives

Edited by Patsy Staddon

First published in Great Britain in 2015 by

Policy Press
University of Bristol
1-9 Old Park Hill
Bristol
BS2 8BB
UK
t: +44 (0)117 954 5940
pp-info@bristol.ac.uk
www.policypress.co.uk

North America office:
Policy Press
c/o The University of Chicago Press
1427 East 60th Street
Chicago, IL 60637, USA
t: +1 773 702 7700
f: +1 773 702 9756
sales@press.uchicago.edu
www.press.uchicago.edu

British Library Cataloguing in Publication Data
A catalogue record for this book is available from the British Library.

Library of Congress Cataloging-in-Publication Data
A catalog record for this book has been requested.

ISBN 978 1 44730 734 1  paperback

Cover design by Policy Press.
Front cover: image kindly supplied by istock
Printed and bound in Great Britain by CMP, Poole
The Policy Press uses environmentally responsible print partners

and is project-managing People and Research West of England, a collaborative approach to public involvement in research across a consortium of universities and NHS organisations in the West of England.

**Steve Gillard** is a mental health services researcher based at St George's, University of London, with extensive experience of supporting and evaluating the impact of service user involvement in mental health research.

**Dr Jayasree Kalathil** is an independent researcher and writer with a background in critical humanities and cultural studies. Her areas of interest and expertise include mental health, race equality and cultural representations of madness. She runs Survivor Research, a virtual collective of researchers interested in issues of racialisation, marginality and equality in mental health. Jayasree is the author of several reports on recovery, user involvement and peer support, including: *Recovery and resilience: African, African Caribbean and South Asian women's narratives about recovering from mental distress* (London: Mental Health Foundation and Survivor Research, 2011); *Dancing to our own tunes: Reassessing Black and Minority Ethnic mental health service user involvement*, Review and Reprint (London: National Survivor User Network, 2011); and *The Sackclothman* (Kottayam: DC Books, 2009). She was one of the two Co-Chairs of the Social Perspectives Network (2009–12) and the editor of *Open Mind* magazine (2010–12).

**Dr Lydia Lewis** is a Research Fellow in the Centre for Developmental and Applied Research in Education at the University of Wolverhampton. She has previously held research posts in Sociology and Education at the Universities of Birmingham, Leicester and Warwick, and a lecturing post in Education Studies (Sociology and Inclusion) at Bath Spa University. She has worked in a knowledge exchange capacity with service user and survivor groups in the area of mental health on a range of projects and through the British Sociological Association Mental Health Study Group, which she founded and co-convenes (see www.britsoc.co.uk/study-groups/sociology-of-mental-health.aspx)

**Professor Hugh McLaughlin** is Professor of Social Work at Manchester Metropolitan University. Before entering academia, Hugh was employed in a range of social service posts, from social worker to Assistant Director (Children and Families). Hugh's research interests include the possibilities and limits of participatory research, critical professional practice, and evidence-informed practice. Hugh is author of *Service-user research in health and social care* (Sage, 2009) and *Understanding social work research* (2nd edn) (Sage, 2009). When not working, Hugh likes to run, read and go scuba-diving.

**Dr Hugh Middleton** is both Clinical Associate Professor of the School of Sociology and Social Policy in Nottingham and an NHS consultant psychiatrist. The latter role provides real world experience of others' mental health difficulties and of services available to provide for them. The former gives an opportunity to reflect upon the issues these raise. His situation has enabled a number of PhD projects which focus on the application of social sciences theory and methods to mental health issues. Hugh has wide experience of the mental health research environment and patient and public involvement in it, having established and – between 2004 and 2008 – led the East Midlands Hub of the UK Mental Health Research Network. He is co-chair of the UK Critical Psychiatry Network.

**Marion Neffgen** is a trainee psychiatrist with specialist experience of working in personality disorders services in the UK. Prior to starting her psychiatry training in London she also worked in psychotherapy in Germany for several years. Marion was working at South West London & St George's Mental Health NHS Trust when this research took place.

**Dr Katherine C. Pollard** is a Senior Research Fellow in the Faculty of Health and Life Sciences, University of the West of England, Bristol, with a clinical background in midwifery. She has particular expertise regarding interprofessional issues and patient and public involvement (PPI) in research processes in health and social care. Recent and current activities include leading a knowledge exchange project to embed PPI routinely in joint research and evaluation activities undertaken by the Faculty and the Severn Deanery, and contributing to an NIHR-funded study exploring the impact of PPI in research on the quality and outcomes of projects. Katherine's presentations about PPI in research include delivering a paper as an invited speaker to the International Health Forum at the University of Ljubljana, Slovenia, as well as discussing researcher perspectives and co-facilitating a workshop with both academics and service users at international conferences in the UK.

**Rachel Purtell** is the Folk.us Director. Folk.us is part of the University of Exeter Medical School. Its role is to ensure that service users, patients and carers are able to have a positive and meaningful impact on research, and the structures and processes that support research in health and social care. Folk.us also supports service users, patients and carers to undertake their own research. Rachel does work with many people, including people with learning difficulties, people who have experienced mental distress, people with physical and/or sensory impairments, older people and people who are long-term users of the NHS. Rachel is also a freelance trainer in Disability Equality Issues using a Social Model of Disability approach and she delivers training for statutory organisations. Rachel is a disabled woman, a disability activist and a service user.

**Dr Wendy Rickard** has worked at Folk.us, University of Exeter Medical School, for four years and is committed to service user involvement in research. Her background is in radical health promotion, public health, oral history and (qualitative) research methodology. She was previously Reader in Public Health Research at the Institute of Public Health and Primary Care, Faculty of Health, London South Bank University and worked closely with the Sound Archive at the British Library. She currently still teaches and supervises postgraduate students in public health at London South Bank University and lectures postgraduates in public history at the Department of History, Royal Holloway College, University of London. Wendy has a small-holding in Devon.

**Dr Patsy Staddon** is a service user and an academic researcher. She developed the concept of a social approach to alcohol use and its treatment, and the sociological implications of current theory and practice in that field, particularly for women and minority groups. She is currently conducting service user-controlled research at the University of Plymouth, funded by Folk.us. She initiated and developed the BSA (British Sociological Association) Alcohol Study Group and is active in service user involvement in research design and analysis and in developing new support mechanisms for women with alcohol issues. She is a member of the Advisory Group of the NIHR's INVOLVE and of NSUN's National (Mental Health) Improvement Programme Advisory Group; Co-Chair of the Social Perspectives of Mental Health Network, and Chair of Women's Independent Alcohol Support (WIAS).

**Dr Angela Sweeney** is a survivor researcher in the Mental Health Sciences Unit at University College London. Her research interests include survivors' perspectives on and experiences of mental health services. She is lead editor of the book *This is survivor research* (2009) and has a PhD in Sociology as applied to Medicine from the Service User Research Enterprise (SURE), Institute of Psychiatry (King's College London). Angela co-convened the seminar series at the British Library from which this book has arisen.

**Kati Turner** is an experienced service user researcher with a lived experience of personality disorder and of using a range of personality disorders services. Kati works as a service user researcher at St George's, University of London, and was chair of the UK peer-led personality disorders organisation Emergence, where she continues to work, at the time of this research project.

# Preface and acknowledgements

It gives me great pride and pleasure to be presenting this book, both for the excellence of its content and for its triumph in bringing together the work of sociologists, 'service users' and 'service user sociologists' to celebrate a unique event and to stand as evidence of the width and depth of service user research and its implications. It was inspired by the seminar series 'Researching in Mental Health: Sociological and Service User/Survivor Perspectives', held at the British Library in 2009 by the Survivor Researcher Network and the British Sociological Association's Sociology of Mental Health Study Group. The series was devised and coordinated by Lydia Lewis, Angela Sweeney, Ruth Sayers and David Armes and included displays of work from two survivor organisations: The Survivor History Group and Recovery. In the introductory chapter, 'Watershed moments in survivor research', Angela Sweeney details how the series came about, and what was entailed; an edited version of the report on it, presented to the Foundation for the Sociology of Health and Illness in July 2009 by Lydia Lewis, is to be found in the Appendix. Special thanks are due to Angela Sweeney and Lydia Lewis not only for their enormous work in the original series, but also for their help to me, as a service user researcher, and a first-time editor, in producing the book.

Eight of the book's chapters are contributed by presenters in the series: Angela Sweeney; Peter Beresford and Kathy Boxall; Hugh Middleton; Steve Gillard, Kati Turner and Marion Neffgen; Lydia Lewis; Patsy Staddon; Jayasree Kalathil; and Sarah Carr. Further academic and service user perspectives on user involvement are added in the chapters by Katherine Pollard and David Evans; Wendy Rickard and Rachel Purtell; and Hugh McLaughlin. In this way, it has been possible to consider the sociological implications of service user involvement and how it may develop in the future.

Many thanks are due to Jude England at the British Library for all her help with the seminar series, and to Karen Bowler, Laura Vickers and Isobel Bainton of The Policy Press for their support with the book's production. I should also like particularly to thank Dr Jackie Barron of the Women's Aid National Office for her unstinting encouragement of me as a new editor in the academic field.

Writers in this book are frequently both academics and service users. Some of us, myself included, feared that our voices would never be heard if we did not acquire some sort of academic status, and often struggled against remarkable odds to achieve this. Some of us outed ourselves from the start, challenging established medical knowledge, as we sought the social perspectives needed to make sense of our worlds. Others hid for years behind academic status, afraid that 'admitting' to a 'service user' identity would disqualify them from serious consideration as academics, and even from employment. This situation is particularly poignant when we consider McLaughlin's point (Chapter Eleven) that we are all likely to be service users one day, and that dividing the world into knowers and their subjects obscures and restricts the very knowledge that is so expensively sought in large-scale research trials, frequently designed without the benefit of a sociological perspective.

In this book, we have issued our own challenges in our own terms, whether as 'service users', colleagues and friends, or both. As Sweeney describes (Chapter One), we began the discussion with the huge achievement of the initial series of seminars at the British Library in 2009. Here, we take a further step, where we criticise and examine the nature and the purpose of service user involvement.

Middleton, for example (Chapter Two), is a consultant psychiatrist who has long condemned the failure of mental health services to listen attentively to what service users are saying. One reason for this inadequate response is, he suggests, the medical model, whereby service users and service providers are notionally separated, using power, privilege and expectation, into one of these two categories. This distinction is fallacious, depending on the long-standing acceptance of the sick role, whereby the 'patient' gives up autonomy in exchange for 'treatment'. Middleton shows how this is an unsuitable model for psychological distress, and how the rise of the service user movement, with its 'service user researchers', challenges and threatens the authorised knowledge based on the sick role. Are there ways in which service user research and service provider research may usefully inform each other and move forward?

Certainly, some researchers have found it possible to make use of collaborative approaches, using a variety of qualitative methodologies, to demonstrate how service user ideals may inform practice. Rickard and Purtell (Chapter Three) use collaborative methods of interviewing and digital storytelling, with service users involved at many levels, and producing knowledge that is narrated in ways that empower those involved. Similarly, Pollard and Evans (Chapter Four) describe the benefits, but also the problematic nature, of full involvement of the public in research, from research question through to dissemination. They discuss the difficulties, such as lack of time, funding, bureaucracy and energy, and the need for opportunities to discuss these so that public involvement can move forward.

Exciting research by Gillard, Turner and Neffgen (Chapter Five) employs methodologies that enable the team, consisting of a service user, a clinician and a researcher, to analyse qualitative data about people with personality disorders. Their approach is reflective and interpretive, with clear benefits, as well as some tensions, shown to develop from working together from their different perspectives and making use of reflective diaries.

In Chapter Six, Beresford, one of the presenters in the series, and Boxall take forward these ideas, showing how collective service user experiential knowledge can transform the way that mental differences and mental distress are understood, bringing to the table understandings of social justice and inequalities, which contribute to the growth of emancipatory research. At the same time, such processes may alarm some 'professionals', lest their own academic position be undermined. The process is both challenging and political.

These political perspectives of service users' impact on, and involvement in, research are fully described and analysed sociologically by Lewis (Chapter Seven). She writes of a 'politics of recognition', whereby the knowledge of women service users in particular is countered by the operation of power dynamics that operate to diminish respect. They are stigmatised by their identity. A similar line of argument is used by Staddon (Chapter Eight), who observes the silencing of alternative discourses for women with alcohol issues. Research in this area is led by moral and medical perspectives that currently appear to go unchallenged by service users too shamed to address the social injustice involved in their position. Kalathil (Chapter Nine) takes a similarly political stance, examining the apparent 'under-representation' of racialised groups in research, and noting the scepticism that has developed among such groups in the wake of unhelpful ways of attempting their involvement, including obvious tokenism. Carr (Chapter Ten) also employs a political and sociological perspective as she describes the ways that lesbian, gay and bisexual people have typically been researched as subjects, with correspondingly skewed findings finding their way into treatment. She proposes better methodologies, particularly auto-ethnography, to document their experiences, and, in so doing, achieve emancipation.

Finally, Hugh McLaughlin (Chapter Eleven) is cautiously optimistic about the ways that service user involvement may develop in the future, whereby we are less fixated on insider knowledge and more interested in a plurality of knowledges. This is a reminder of Beresford and Boxall's observations in Chapter Six.

I bring the book to a close with some brief reflections of my own on how the book reveals the ways that knowledge is constructed, and its role in the expression and redistribution of power. Are we indeed stuck irrevocably in a relationship whereby such power belongs with established and vested academic interests, and the service user, whether seen as a 'subject' or merely as a useful adjunct to acquiring research funding, is denied access to the decisions as to who is funded, to do what and why?

*Patsy Staddon, 2013*

# ONE

# Sociology and survivor research: an introduction

*Angela Sweeney*

## Watershed moments in survivor research

Survivor research is a relatively new form of service user activism. It formalises the desire of psychiatric system users and survivors to generate our own knowledge about our experiences. In its short history – little more than 20 years – survivor research has had a number of watershed moments. These include the publication of the directly challenging *Have we got views for you* (Beeforth et al, 1994) and the development of the first national survivor-controlled research programmes, User Focused Monitoring (Rose, 2001) and Strategies for Living (Faulkner and Layzell, 1999), in the late 1990s. More recently, the publication of the survivor-edited *This is survivor research* (Sweeney et al, 2009) demonstrated just how far survivor research has travelled. A seminar series at the British Library, also in 2009 – from which this book has emerged – represents another key milestone.

Entitled 'Researching in Mental Health: Sociological and Service User/Survivor Perspectives', the series was convened by a sociologist, Lydia Lewis, and three survivor researchers, Ruth Sayers, David Armes and myself.[1] The aim of the seminar series was to promote dialogue, debate and mutual learning between sociologists and survivor researchers. Around 40 people from as far afield as Northern Ireland, France and Germany attended each seminar. Delegates came from a wide variety of backgrounds, including service users and survivors who had and had not been involved in research, sociologists, clinical academics, mental health researchers, and practising clinicians. Each seminar was accompanied by display stands from two survivor-controlled organisations, the Survivor History Group and Recovery. The series was a rare platform to share examples of survivor-controlled research. But it was also a unique opportunity to explore the similarities and differences between survivor research and sociological research, to establish common ground, and to expose and debate fracture points. As stated, this book emerged directly from the seminar series.

## Sociology and survivors' voices

Sociology has a strong tradition of representing the lives of people who are marginalised within society, and the history of the discipline is littered with classic texts which do just that. For instance, William Foote Whyte's (1955 [1943]) *Street corner society*, first published in 1943, sought to understand and represent the rich social world of underprivileged young boys and men in a Boston slum. Foote Whyte was an exponent of participant observation in urban sociology, a method he used to get closer to the experiences of the individuals and groups he studied. In explaining his research to a key participant, Foote Whyte commented: 'I felt I could do very little as an outsider. Only if I could get to know the people and learn their problems first hand would I be able to gain the understanding I needed' (Foote Whyte, 1955 [1943], p 291). The resultant work demonstrates how the social worlds of those who are rarely heard can be explored and portrayed. Yet, while the voices of those within the text are strong, they are represented through the lens of an academic researcher who participated in and observed their social world in order to share it, along with its sociological implications, with the academic world.

The tendency to represent the voices of the marginalised through the lens of detached academic interpretation is also seen in the sociology of mental health and distress. For example, one of the greatest classical sociological texts is Erving Goffman's (1961) *Asylums*. In it, Goffman introduces the concept of institutionalisation by exploring the asylum from the perspective of its inmates. This was significant in bringing about deinstitutionalisation (the closure of Victorian asylums and their replacement with community care), meaning that Goffman's theory has had an immense and ongoing impact on people's lives. Beyond *Asylums*, there are numerous sociological theories about psychiatric service users and our experiences that are deeply valuable in illuminating the social conditions that create and compound mental distress, among them, inhumane treatments, iatrogenesis, poverty, labelling, inequality and discrimination. Yet, while these sociological theories are of great importance, often contributing to improvements in our lives, none have come from survivors:

> we have never developed our own theory of madness and distress to underpin our research work. In its absence,

> different theories *about* us continue to be created, some of
> which come closer to understanding our experiences than
> others. We tend to favour some of these and to reject others
> but none of these theories have come from a systematic
> and thorough investigation of our own knowledge. (Russo,
> 2012, p 33, emphasis in original)

In recent years, there has been some focus on lay perspectives within medical sociology. For instance, in the 1999 edition of *A sociology of mental health and illness* (Pilgrim and Rogers, 1999), a number of standpoints on mental health from within and beyond sociology were explained. Perspectives inside sociology included major theories such as social causation and social realism, while those on the outside of sociology were described as lay perspectives, psychiatry, psychoanalysis, psychology and the legal framework. Survivor testimonies such as *Speaking our minds* (Read and Reynolds, 1996) and *From the ashes of experience* (Barker et al, 1999) or the flourishing survivor-led research programmes at the Mental Health Foundation and (then Sainsbury) Centre for Mental Health were not mentioned. While lay perspectives and survivor accounts are not synonymous – largely because lay experts do not necessarily have personal experience – it is worth exploring some reactions to lay perspectives by medical sociologists because these expose some of the ways that sociology and survivors might engage.

One example is Turner's (2001) discussion of the nature of expertise. While the discussion includes a classification of experts, it fails to consider lay expertise, experiential knowledge or expertise by experience. Thus, the concepts of lay expertise and expertise by experience are often ignored by medical sociologists. More explicitly, Prior (2003) has questioned the increasing role of lay expertise in medical sociology. She argues that 'the concept of lay expert is an oxymoron' because lay people are not skilled or practised in diagnosing and managing illness, are experts in their particular case only, and can be plain wrong: 'Indeed, it is only by virtue of "having experience" that we can even begin to think of such a creature as a lay expert' (Prior, 2003, p 53). Prior continues:

> all in all, they are experts by virtue of 'having experience'. Yet,
> experience on its own is rarely sufficient to understand the
> technical complexities of disease causation, its consequences
> or its management. This is partly because experiential
> knowledge is invariably limited, and idiosyncratic. It
> generates knowledge about the one instance, the one case,

the single 'candidate'.... Above all, lay people can be wrong. (Prior, 2003)

Experiential knowledge – the knowledge that comes from the exploration of individual and shared experiences – is the bedrock of survivor research. The arguments that this knowledge is partial, individual and limited to one's own self-care mean that survivor research, as well as lay expertise, can be subject to wholesale rejection.

We have seen two reactions to lay expertise and, by extension, survivor research within sociology: being overlooked, as in Turner's (2001) work; and being rejected, as in Prior's arguments. Within single research studies, Pilgrim and Rogers (1999) have outlined four main ways in which survivors' voices are silenced:

- Survivors' views are disregarded where they do not coincide with professionals' views.
- Survivors are seen as consistently irrational and therefore unable to give valid views.
- Professionals assume that service users, survivors and relatives share opinions, and where they conflict, service users' views are ignored.
- Survivors' views are reframed to coincide with professionals' views.

Survivor research is one way of enabling the voices of service users and survivors to be heard.

## Reclaiming our voices

In their exploration of service user- and survivor-controlled research, Turner and Beresford (2005) found that there can be an unspoken yet pervasive discrimination at work, which mirrors the silencing and dismissal of lay experts:

> Service users ... felt there were negative often discriminatory responses to user controlled research. But these rarely surface in formal discussions and published literature. They are instead part of a hidden history of user controlled research, usually only finding expression in informal and unrecorded discussions among researchers or with service user researchers, or in the confidential and anonymised statements of peer reviewers, grant assessors and so on. (Turner and Beresford, 2005, p 11)

While many marginalised groups have had their experiences explored and represented by academic sociologists – such as the boys and young men in Foote Whyte's (1955 [1943]) study – for mental health survivors, this can be particularly noxious and damaging. This is because, historically, our experiences have been disbelieved or dismissed, while our distress has been reduced to symptoms of a psychiatric condition. This 'medicalisation of misery' causes direct damage through, for example, discrimination, social exclusion and invasive and harmful treatments such as psychopharmacology and Electro-convulsive Therapy (ECT). Simply being given a psychiatric diagnosis can result in our knowledge and experiences being dismissed as irrational, illogical, mad, extreme and emotional (Rose, 2003). This excludes survivors' voices from mainstream knowledge production, including sociology.

Survivor research directly challenges the silencing and exclusion of service user and survivor voices from mainstream research. In doing so, survivor researchers also challenge the sociological tradition of understanding and representing our worlds through the lens of detached academic interpretation. Peter Beresford has written extensively about the role and value of experience in knowledge generation, arguing that: 'The greater the distance between direct experience and its interpretation, then the more likely resulting knowledge is to be inaccurate, unreliable and distorted' (Beresford, 2003, p 4).

Beresford believes that survivor researchers need to reclaim and re-explore the role and value of first-hand experience. Of course, Beresford argues, such experience is inherently individual: we can interpret our own experiences in different ways at different times, with different people potentially having different interpretations of the same experience. Rather than using this to reject the role of experiential knowledge, as argued by Prior, we should instead seek ways of including range and diversity, and of synthesising individual experiences into collective understandings of commonalities and differences. To do this, Beresford argues that we must explore what distances us from our experiences and how we get closer to them.

This does not mean that survivors alone can understand and represent experiences, although Beresford is clear that the knowledge of others should never be privileged over that of survivors. Instead, others are able to get closer to the experiences of survivors through having similar experiences, for example, of marginalisation or of caring, and through ascribing to a set of value-based principles. Thus, Beresford's fundamental hypothesis is not how we can achieve neutrality, objectivity and distance, but how we can give the subjective centre stage in research-generated knowledge.

Survivor research, then, is a medium through which we represent ourselves and our own voices, and generate our own knowledge. Many of the chapters in this book are testament to the power of exploring social phenomena through direct personal experience. For instance, Patsy Staddon draws on personal experiences, primary research with women who use alcohol and sociological writings to consider the development of a social model of alcohol use that directly challenges biomedical models of alcoholism and addiction.

## Conversations on a new footing: the significance of the British Library seminar series

I began by stating that the joint survivor and sociologist seminar series at the British Library represented a key milestone in the history of survivor research. This is because, despite the marginalisation of survivor research (eg through insecure and infrequent funding, dismissal, and discrimination; see Beresford, 2009), survivor and mainstream sociological researchers were able to come together *on equal terms*. There are few platforms for survivor researchers to explore and express our methods and findings, and even fewer for us to share these with other academics. The seminars were a unique and rare opportunity to showcase our research and discuss it with a large and diverse audience. Presenting survivor research alongside more traditional sociological research enabled us to explore similarities and fissures, often through lively and engaging debates and ongoing conversations. But perhaps most significantly, the seminar series gave our work a new legitimacy by directly challenging unspoken discrimination and assumptions about survivor research. Doing so in the eminent surroundings of the British Library seemed to compound this sense of legitimacy. Rather than being examined, investigated or explored, mental health system users and survivors were able to speak for ourselves.

The seminar series was also testament to the journey that sociology has undertaken. From the radical urban sociologists who investigated the social worlds of the marginalised through participant observation to contemporary medical sociologists who acknowledge, albeit with dissent, the role of lay experts, sociologists are now acknowledging the power of participatory and survivor-controlled research and are beginning to engage with survivors on an equal footing. Many of the chapters in this book demonstrate the ways in which sociologists are embracing issues of voice and representation and the implications this has for research and practice. For example, Hugh Middleton's reflections on the epistemological assumptions that underpin mental health services is revealing about the positioning of service users and survivors in knowledge production, while Katherine Pollard and David Evans reflect on the involvement of service users and survivors in research from their perspectives as (non-survivor) academics.

However, there is still some way for us to travel: 'As far as the dominant debate is concerned, survivors and the survivors' movement still seem to be primarily seen as a source of experiential data, rather than creators of our own analysis and theory' (Beresford and Wallcraft, 1997, quoted in Russo, 2012).

This can make it hard for us to influence sociological debates that typically take place in the arena of theory. As survivors such as Russo and Beresford have argued, survivor researchers must develop our own theories in order to truly reclaim our voices and thereby engage with sociologists on equal terms. At present, survivors are exploring the possibility of a social model of madness and distress (Beresford, 2010; Beresford et al, 2010). This is a complex undertaking, but an exciting one. Given the new legitimacy of survivors' accounts within sociology, sociologists should be uniquely positioned to engage with these survivor-generated models of madness and distress.

## Acknowledgements

The British Library seminar series was funded by the Foundation for the Sociology of Health and Illness. The idea for the series came from Dr David Armes. Special thanks are due to Dr Lydia Lewis for her work in securing funding and organising the series. The series was administrated by the British Sociological Association, with special thanks due to Liz Jackson and Michelle Rhone. Thanks are also due to Dr Jude England, Head of Social Science Collections and Research, for her interest, enthusiasm and support.

## Note

[1] Coordinators came from and were supported by the British Sociological Association, Medical Sociology Group, Sociology of Mental Health Study Group and the Survivor Researcher Network.

## References

Barker, P., Campbell, P. and Davidson, B. (eds) (1999) *From the ashes of experience: reflections on madness, survival and growth*, London: Whurr.

Beeforth, M., Conlan, E. and Graley, R. (1994) *Have we got views for you: user evaluation of case management*, London: The Centre for Mental Health.

Beresford, P. (2003) *It's our lives: a short theory of knowledge, distance and experience*, London: OSP for Citizens Press in Association with Shaping Our Lives.

Beresford, P. (2009) 'Control', in J. Wallcraft, B. Schrank and M. Amering (eds) *Handbook of service user involvement in mental health research*, Chichester: John Wiley & Sons, pp 181–97.

Beresford, P. (2010) 'A straight talking introduction to being a mental health service user', in R. Bentall and P. Sanders (eds) *Straight talking introduction to mental health problems*, Ross-on-Wye: PCCS.

Beresford, P. and Wallcraft, J. (1997) 'Psychiatric system survivors and emancipatory research: issues, overlaps and differences', in C. Barnes and G. Mercer (eds) *Doing disability research*, Leeds: The Disability Press, pp 66–87.

Beresford, P., Nettle, M. and Perring, R. (2010) *Towards a social model of madness and distress? Exploring what service users say*, York: Joseph Rowntree Foundation.

Faulkner, A. and Layzell, S. (1999) *Strategies for Living: A report on user-led research*, London: The Mental Health Foundation

Foote Whyte, W. (1955 [1943]) *Street corner society: the social structure of an Italian slum* (2nd edn), Chicago, IL: Chicago Press.

Goffman, E. (1961) *Asylums: essays on the social situation of mental patients and other inmates*, Oxford: Doubleday (Anchor).

Pilgrim, D. and Rogers, A. (1999) *A sociology of mental health and illness* (2nd edn), Buckingham and Philadelphia, PA: Open University Press.

Prior, L. (2003) 'Belief, knowledge and expertise: the emergence of the lay expert in medical sociology', *Sociology of Health & Illness*, vol 25, no 3, pp 41–57.

Read, J. and Reynolds, J. (eds) (1996) *Speaking our minds: an anthology of personal experience of mental distress and its consequences*, Basingstoke: Macmillan/Open University Press.

Rose, D. (2001) *Users' voices: the perspectives of mental health service users on community and hospital care*, London: Sainsbury Centre for Mental Health.

Rose, D. (2003) 'Collaborative research between users and professionals: peaks and pitfalls', *Psychiatric Bulletin*, vol 27, pp 404–6.

Russo, J. (2012) 'Survivor-controlled research: a new foundation for thinking about psychiatry and mental health', *Forum: Qualitative Social Research*, vol 13, no 1, Art 8.

Sweeney, A., Beresford, P., Faulkner, A., Nettle, M. and Rose, D. (eds) (2009) *This is survivor research*, Ross-on-Wye: PCCS.

Turner, M. and Beresford, P. (2005) *User controlled research: its meaning and potential*, Eastleigh: INVOLVE Support Unit.

Turner, S. (2001) 'What is the problem with experts?', *Social Studies of Science*, vol 31, no 1, pp 123–49.

## TWO

# Mental health service users' experiences and epistemological fallacy

### Hugh Middleton

This chapter offers a perspective of mental health service users' experiences of research from one who is not a mental health service user. Some 20 years as a consultant psychiatrist in the UK NHS have provided their own rich and intimate familiarity with mental health services and the experiences of those who use them. I am convinced that much can be gained for all concerned by respecting those experiences in much more detail. I know that I am not alone in this. However, this collection and related publications are testimony to widespread frustration that it is not happening quickly enough. Continuing failure to incorporate non-medical approaches into mental health services' policy, practice and research are experienced as oppressive and harmful. The value of a social perspective on 'mental health difficulties', the services available to provide for them and the research upon which they are purported to be based is compelling. Of particular interest to a social scientist is the need to understand the nature and background of this resistance to change.

One approach to this is to consider the causes and implications of locating 'mental health difficulties' in a 'medical illness' framework. From a historical perspective, this is a relatively recent development, but it has become virtually universal, and defines participants' roles and power relations in ways that influence their expectations of research. The 'medical illness' framework imposes a distinction between 'service user' and 'service provider', generating distinct communities of discourse. Experiences within these distinct communities of discourse generate distinct forms of knowledge, and it is, of course, the relative contributions of these to even wider discourse that determines the power relation between them. Thus, to what extent, from this point of view, are service users' perspectives truly distinct, or are they better understood as a reflection of the arbitrary (though long-standing) distinction between 'users' and 'providers'? Are both communities better understood as component parts of a larger whole? To what extent is it an epistemological fallacy to talk in terms of service users' experiences when service users and service providers are both entwined in a dance where both play their parts, albeit with different experiences of power and privilege? To what extent should, and does, research enlighten understanding of this mutuality, and what are the limits and constraints upon liberation from the oppression and inequalities that it entails?

## Folie et déraison

This approach draws heavily on the work of Michel Foucault. *Folie et déraison: histoire de la folie à l'âge classique*, his first major book and doctoral thesis, was initially published in French in 1961. My source is the 2007 edition of Richard Howard's 1967 English translation, based on the abridged edition published in 1964 (Foucault, 2007 [1964]). *Folie et déraison* examines ideas, practices and institutional responses to 'madness' from the early Enlightenment to the modern era. It describes ways in which a variety of metaphors have been used across time to describe and justify the social exclusion and confinement of the disturbing, the threatening or the merely inconvenient. The historical narrative ends with Sigmund Freud and medically administered psychoanalysis. It outlines how Tuke's and Pinel's work, generally presented as liberating, can be seen to have ushered in our most modern form of alienation and oppression, whereby 'madness' becomes an affliction to be treated, and the 'mad', aliens to be acted upon:

> To the doctor, Freud transferred all the structures Pinel and Tuke had set up within confinement. He did deliver the patient from the existence of the asylum within which his 'liberators' had alienated him; but he did not deliver him from what was essential in this existence; he regrouped its powers, extended them to the maximum by uniting them in the doctor's hands; he created the psychoanalytical situation where, by an inspired short-circuit, alienation becomes disalienating because, in the doctor, it becomes a subject. (Foucault, 2007 [1964], p 264)

As Foucault's historical account ends in the 1950s, it does not and could not include an account of the last half-century, during which, in Euro-American settings, a discourse identifying 'madness' as an illness to be treated by experts in specialised settings and facilities has become consolidated. Landmarks of this period include a shift of emphasis to provision in community settings and the proliferation of psychopharmacological treatments. They also include changes in mental health legislation that oblige even those not considered sufficiently 'at risk' to require detention and to submit themselves to medical treatment and supervision. In parallel, the view that 'madness' is a collection of illnesses to be treated by professionals as in any other field of medical endeavour has become a dominant public discourse.

## The classic sick role

To consider a state of affairs an 'illness' is a very specific and influential step. It identifies the condition as a particular form of deviance and specifies related power relations. Although frequently criticised, Parsons's (1951) outline of the sick role has stood the test of time and remains an effective summary of this process. Simon Williams provides a contemporary outline of the balance of rights and responsibilities entailed in the classic sick role:

> From the point of view of the social system, too low a level of health and too high an incidence of illness is dysfunctional. Illness, in other words, given its interference with normal role capacity, becomes a form of social deviance that needs channelling therefore in an appropriate fashion through an institutionalized role or niche. The sick role, for Parsons, fulfils precisely these goals through a series of rights and obligations that its incumbents must recognize and respect. On the rights side of the equation, the patient (according to the severity of the illness) is exempt from normal role obligations, and is not deemed responsible for falling ill. On the obligations side of the equation, the patient must seek technically competent help and must want to get well. The doctor, for his part, must apply these technically competent skills in order to facilitate (a swift) recovery, guided as he is by the professional constellation of achievement, universalism, functional specificity, affective neutrality and collectivity-orientation.
>
> The sick role, therefore, serves to discourage the secondary gains of illness and prevent what Parsons, rightly or wrongly, sees as a deviant subculture of sickness from forming through this reciprocal cluster of rights and obligations, the aim of which is to reintegrate the individual back into society through a return to normal role capacity (or an

approximation thereof) as quickly as possible. (Williams, 2005, p 124)

'Illness' is considered a form of deviance, but by providing an institutional response to it, the social system negotiates a highly specific contract. The 'ill' person enjoys relief from responsibilities and access to care in exchange for a resignation of authority, submission to expertly defined treatment and dependency upon others. The ill person may resign command over most of their affairs, but they still have power over others in the form of expectations of care and support. The ill person also gives up their right to assumptions of full competence and is at risk of assumptions of incapacity or incompetence. Despite criticisms and its origins in classic social theory, this interpretation of observable structural and relational arrangements retains considerable explanatory power. However, substantive criticisms do gather strength when they are applied to circumstances that do not conform to a narrowly stereotyped expression of illness.

## Differing expressions of illness

Before the widespread introduction of sterile surgical techniques, effective antibiotics and immunisation during the second half of the 19th and first half of the 20th century, life-threatening illness commonly took the form of an acutely debilitating fever due to bacterial infection, such as pneumonia, puerperal sepsis or septicaemia from a gangrenous wound. Until recent times, common experience of serious illness was that of a fever that either 'broke', in other words, resolved as the body's natural defences prevailed, or resulted in death. During the fever, the victim would be incapacitated by pain and weakness, and personal hygiene, nutrition and fluid intake would have to be supported by others. Under such circumstances, it is clearly adaptive to deploy an institutionalised interaction between 'patient' and 'carers' in which the 'patient' temporarily surrenders autonomy in return for the professional care and support that are realistically likely to improve their outcome, perhaps even save their life. This may have even greater antiquity, reflecting the biological efficiencies of intensively caring for a relatively small number of dependent young that is characteristic of mammals, or a parent–child relationship if viewed from a psychodynamic perspective. Nevertheless, however well suited it might be for expressions of illness that conform to historically prevalent stereotypes, there are limits to the validity of the classic sick role in relation to other expressions of 'illness' that have arisen in modern times.

With the development of sterile surgical techniques and the availability of antibiotics, survival after serious injury such as spinal transaction causing paralysis, loss of a limb or a brain-damaging head injury have become much more likely than was the case less than a few generations ago. Mortality following surgical amputation of a limb stood at around 60% in the early 19th century; by 1910, it had fallen to some 10% (Alexander, 1985). The need to accommodate the 'disabled but no longer ill' is a relatively new development. It has only recently found full expression in the form of disability rights legislation, and it has taken much of the 20th century for related legislative and attitudinal changes to mature. Specifically, these include redeeming the disabled from the status of 'patronised and dependent person' characteristic of a patient inhabiting the classic sick role to that of 'autonomous and independent person' with full expectations of rights and responsibilities. In more recent decades, medical developments have altered the prognosis of many other conditions from 'certainly very disabling and commonly life-threatening' to 'manageable provided certain regimes are followed'. Examples of this include diabetes, hypertension, asthma and epilepsy. Over a period of little more than 150 years, the everyday experience of serious illness has widened from that of a time-limited episode resulting in either recovery or death, to one that includes chronic physical disability, the presence of a persistent threat of life-endangering recurrence despite ongoing well-being (as in cancer in remission), steadily declining health beyond the reach of professional skills (such as the experience of progressive arthritis) and continuing well-being contingent upon a programme of professionalised intervention (such as controlled diabetes, asthma, hypertension or epilepsy). None of these are adequately accommodated by the classic sick role and all of them present challenges to the oversimplification it represents. Nevertheless, it has deep historical roots and it is a resilient social structure. It orders and legitimises influential institutions and power relations. When it is applied to situations that do not match its historical template, these may be unhelpful. Related power relations lose their legitimacy and the scene is set for tensions and dissatisfactions. Although these have begun to influence practice and have stimulated the introduction of supportive legislation in relation to physical conditions, the same has yet to happen with any measure in the mental health field. Thus, mental health service users experience institutions, practices and power relations that commonly reflect the ill-suited application of social arrangements derived from an archaic social response to 'illness'.

## Mental 'illness'?

Foucault suggests that adoption of an illness metaphor for 'mental disorder' was not the humanitarian advance that it has generally been considered. In his view, before this, 'the mad' had been viewed as inherently flawed persons in need of paternalistically provided care in segregated settings. For Foucault, adoption of the illness metaphor during the first half of the 20th century, in the form of psychoanalytic psychotherapy, but also, at the same time, in the forms of shock therapy and leucotomy, did not deny the notion of a flawed person any more than 'heart failure' denies the perception of a flawed body. What it did do was consolidate the dynamics of the classic sick role into understandings of the social arrangements available to accommodate 'the mad'. As these are historically deep-rooted and therefore very influential, they have played a major part in shaping mental health services and power relations among those participating in them. They legitimise and encourage certain interests and they oblige actors to conform to particular roles and expectations. As 'mental health difficulties' only occasionally fit specifications of situations suiting the classic sick role, this can be experienced as oppressive, constraining or exploitative by one or more of the participating actors.

One illustration is an article published in 1982 and charmingly entitled 'Chancers, pests and poor wee souls: problems of legitimation in psychiatric nursing' (May and Kelly, 1982). Relationships between in-patient psychiatric nurses and their charges were used to comment upon the occupation of psychiatric nursing. As commonly happens, certain 'patients' were identified as 'problem patients'. May and Kelly were able to show that such individuals were those who challenged the validity of nurses' therapeutic authority. They were those whose needs and behaviours were not readily accommodated by specifications of the classic sick role. Such patients' reasons for being in hospital were not easily attributed to a clearly defined diagnosis. Their expectations of staff went beyond the limits of what might be expected of a professional working in that context. They were unwilling to accept the submissive role usually expected of a 'patient'. They made practical or emotional demands that could not be fulfilled within the conceptual framework of an incapacitated person in legitimate need of assistance. They challenged the applicability of the classic sick role to their needs. 'Patients' experienced a reluctance to acknowledge their concerns, and providers experienced unjustified or seemingly inappropriate expectations of entitlement normally associated with the sick role.

Satisfactory relations between mental health service users and mental health service providers depend upon both adhering to a particular code of conduct. The 'rules' of conduct are set by long-standing and widely accepted conventions. The identities of 'service user' and 'service provider' are functions of these conventions. Their validity is no greater than the applicability of the sick role to the purpose of their interaction. In the many contested situations where 'users' experience inappropriate paternalism and 'providers' experience unwelcome intrusion, the particular roles and identities of 'user' and 'provider' are being forced upon a situation that does not suit them. The role of 'user' or 'patient' comes with expectations of privileged access to resources and the role of 'provider' or 'professional' comes with expectations of power and authority. This supports productive collaboration when the task is the provision of expert care for one temporarily limited in their ability to care for themselves. However, it becomes a source of conflict if the task is otherwise, such as the conduct of a research project. On the other hand, in common with any other dialectic, such conflict also has the potential to generate truly new knowledge. For that to happen, however, each contender has to understand the other's position and recognise the contextual determinants of their own. As is common where there are differences of material power and status, this is hindered by politically apparent group processes: counterproductive stereotyping and defensive posturing. These interfere with the development of a middle ground where both positions have validity and co-produced knowledge can develop.

## Sick roles and research roles

My suggestion is that the distinct identities of 'mental health service user researcher' and 'professional mental health researcher' reflect the template identities of 'patient' and 'professional' defined by the classic sick role. This is unsatisfactory because provisions of the classic sick role suit very few, if any, instances of so-called mental illness. Furthermore, the task of a research project is not that of caring for an afflicted person, but that of generating new knowledge. Many service users have found therapeutic benefit from participation in research, but it is arguable that such benefit would have followed participation in any activity capable of providing empowerment, emancipation, esteem, learning or personal growth. Any one of these may have been potentiated by labelling the activity 'research', but the fact that it led to therapeutic benefit has to be independent of whether or not the activity led to new knowledge, other than participants' understandings of themselves.

Obtaining research funds from competitive sources is part of what marks a successful academic career. The pursuit of empowerment, emancipation (from junior status), esteem, learning and other forms of personal growth is not restricted to the so-called recovery journey. Self-realisation can be seen just as clearly when a successful academic achieves their ambitions as when someone recovers from a period of 'mental illness' through participation in a research project. How they differ is in the extent and nature of the opportunities they have to hand. Among medical (and mental health) researchers, these are simultaneously considerable and narrowly restricted. Opportunities are considerable because medical research is highly valued, heavily resourced and widely respected. In exactly the same way that the classic sick role endorses appropriate and professionally administered care of the sick, productive medical research is lauded as of unquestioned merit. Thus, governments, universities and charitable bodies all make money available. Commercial organisations justify their expansion and the promotion of expensive new treatments for similar reasons, and medical 'breakthroughs' are popular news stories. Conversely, opportunities are also narrowly restricted. Medical research has to conform to very specific limitations, and these also reflect parameters of the classic sick role. The doctor (or any other professional health care practitioner) only holds authority over a submissive patient because they are considered to hold expert knowledge and can access facilities denied to others. These privileges are won by joining an elite through study, apprenticeship and explicit agreement to conform to a code of conduct. This is generally viewed as a means of protecting patients from impropriety and exploitation, but it also constrains the practitioner's freedom and scope for creativity. Regulatory bodies censure practitioners who recommend courses of action that do not conform to professionally agreed opinion, even when there are no concerns over propriety or exploitation. One example of this might be the controversy over the acceptability of prayer in contemporary health care settings (Hope, 2009).

It is convention to resolve such controversies by reference to 'evidence-based' practice. This refers to censure and financial discipline encouraging practitioners to only use treatments and other courses of action that have been recommended by advisory bodies who base their recommendations upon academic review of the scientific literature and other sources of 'expert opinion'. In the UK, these are developed by the National Institute for Health and Clinical Excellence (NICE) and disseminated as NICE Guidelines, which specify what the NHS can and cannot be expected to provide. In other jurisdictions, where health care is funded through insurance organisations, comparable arrangements exist to ensure that only similarly agreed programmes of treatment are remunerated.

The medical scientific literature and 'expert opinion' are the same sources of knowledge and authority that legitimise the role of patronising professional in enactments of the classic sick role. However privileged and autonomous the practitioner might appear to be, they are but a purveyor of an authorised and established body of knowledge. This is presented as definitive and authoritative, but only because it is shared and agreed by the very same established bodies that enjoy access to it and the privileges that it bestows. These constraints upon what knowledge is included in the repertoire of 'evidence' that authorises practice and what knowledge is not are keenly reflected in how it is generated and shared – in how research is commissioned. If information is to become part of established medical knowledge – the basis of an approved treatment and thereby a remunerable act of health care – then it has to belong.

This is illustrated by the well-known evidence hierarchy (Gray, 1997), which ranges from meta-analysis of randomised controlled clinical trials to 'expert opinion'. If there is no clinical trial data available to evaluate a particular treatment, 'expert opinion' is an acceptable substitute, but there is no place for any other form of opinion. The epistemological rigour of 'evidence-based medicine' is not unquestioned (Worrall, 2010), but it does exert a defining influence upon the funding and conduct of medical research, and the activities and interests of the professional medical research community. Funding organisations, whether statutory, charitable or commercial, tend to focus support upon research likely to influence practice. As practice reflects a particular corpus of knowledge, they only fund research that will contribute to it. Other forms of knowledge, such as those informing relationships, values, experiences and meanings, do not, in general, contribute to the established corpus of medical knowledge. As a result, they cannot formally contribute to the specialised knowledge and skills base that authorise the practitioner's place in the actions of the classic sick role, and, thereby, carry little weight in the competitive world of medical research grant-winning, or in the advancement of professional research careers.

The 'service user researcher' stands in an entirely different place on this field. Their part in the classic sick role is an unsteady balance between oppression and power. In an archetypal doctor–patient relationship, patients relinquish autonomy and subject themselves to the doctor's will. At the same time, they move to occupy the centre of the doctor's gaze, and, in doing so, acquire and can exert ultimate power over the course of the interaction. The patient may be obliged to respect the authority of the doctor's knowledge, skills and status, and relinquish autonomy over some or all of their actions. The doctor's knowledge and skills may be unquestioned, provided that they are executed in pursuit of the patient's recovery and conform to agreed practice. The patient is, however, the ultimate arbiter. Only they (or their organs) can pass judgement upon the success of the doctor's endeavours.

Furthermore, the classic sick role prescribes different levels of investment by 'service user' and by 'service provider'. No honourable practitioner would fully subscribe to the statement 'The operation was a success, but unfortunately the patient died', but many would recognise the uncomfortable tensions between doing everything professionally expected of them and being unable to meet expectations. Formally, the service provider's role is limited to carrying out professional responsibilities within limits set by their professional canon. The service user has much more invested. This particular illness or episode of difficulties is a singular and specific situation that can only be adequately understood in the context of their own personal narrative and relationships. Although the classic sick role may be adequate for the archetypal situation in which the condition is debilitating and short-lived and for which there is a clearly defined and potentially effective treatment, when these conditions are not met and it cannot effectively contain events, it is incompletely understood without recourse to other sources of knowledge. These include those derived from direct experience of the condition and its treatment. They lie beyond the reach of accredited 'professional' knowledge. In situations where the classic sick role is a sufficient framework, such knowledge might be of peripheral interest. In situations where it is inadequate, such knowledge may be central.

## Implications for 'mental health' research

To summarise: the classic sick role continues to exert a defining influence over all aspects of health care. Despite its limited applicability in relation to many modern expressions of 'illness', it retains considerable discursive resilience, and this extends into the politics of medical research. Patterns of reward and institutional arrangements reflect the actions of powerful interest groups, which draw their authority from the classic sick role, and this is based in part upon the view that knowledge held and exercised by a privileged few is a key commodity.

Foucault felt that espousal of the illness metaphor by those concerned with the 'mad' was not the humanitarian advance that it is generally considered to have been. More than 50 years on, it is worth reflecting once more on how well 'mental illnesses' conform to expectations of the classic sick role, and the power relations that come with it:

- Conventionally, 'mental illnesses' are not considered periods of temporary incapacity. Levels of disability might fluctuate, but most, if not all, are considered, by professionals, to be evidence of enduring vulnerability.
- 'Mental illnesses' are not stable entities similarly apparent to lay and professional observers alike. The 1970s and 1980s saw considerable investment in developing detailed diagnostic criteria. They have proved unstable and of limited clinical value (Middleton, 2008).
- There is little agreement over how any one 'mental illness' might be understood. Someone suffering from the common affliction of recurrent panic attacks might be considered to have disturbed brain chemistry, catastrophic misinterpretations, psycho-developmental issues or stress, depending upon the consulting professional's theoretical leanings. Thus, there is no authoritative view shared by all concerned, derived from an agreed and authoritative body of professional opinion.
- There is equally little consensus over treatment. Despite some 50 years of investment in psychopharmacology research and loudly trumpeted 'advances', it is now clear that there are no differences in effectiveness among the so-called antidepressants or among the so-called antipsychotics, and when they do work, we do not know why (Moncrieff, 2008). The same is broadly true for psychological treatments. A major review of some 3,000 cases has established that the most influential component of the psychological treatments they had received was the quality of the relationship with the therapist (Stiles et al, 2008).

## Epistemological fallacy

It is perhaps unsurprising to conclude that mental health difficulties do not fit into the classic sick role framework. A full account of the consequences and reasons behind trying to hammer the round peg of 'mental health difficulties' into the square hole of 'illness to be treated' is another piece of work. They do, however, point to a potentially helpful way of accounting for the difficulties experienced by certain 'service user researchers'. Considering a state of affairs as an 'illness to be treated' constrains the way that it is viewed and defines the roles and relationships among the participants. These are defined by the discursively robust classic sick role, which can be caricatured as a parent–child relationship. It infantilises the value of knowledge that does not contribute to the 'grown-up' world of science and clinical trials, where grants are won, careers are developed and the conventional 'evidence base' is extended. It obliges 'professional researchers' to present their activities as 'in the patients' interests', even when they are not and doing so is transparently patronising.

In contrast, 'user researchers' are driven to adopt angry, petulant or dismissive postures, or obliged to submit to *force majeure*. None of these are helpful, and all overlook the fact that research conducted from any of these positions is epistemologically naive. Knowledge of any sort is a co-construction. Institutional derivatives of the classic sick role create artificial distinctions between 'service user' and 'service provider' that hinder this. Until such distinctions can be transcended, all research remains suffixed by 'from a service user's perspective' or 'from a service provider's perspective', and is of only limited value. It is naive to imagine that service user input into a research project designed to capture funding from conventional sources by promising to add to the store of conventional knowledge will improve upon what 'professional researchers' might have achieved. It is equally naive to argue that anything is gained, in terms of improving provision for the distressed, despairing, confused and anxiety-provoking, by simply adding to the store of knowledge buttressing a medical perspective.

There is an urgent need to find better ways of responding to distressing levels of human difficulty than merely alienating the afflicted. Alienation, whether it be by labelling the difficulty 'demonic possession', 'lunacy', 'moral degeneracy', 'schizophrenia', 'depression' or 'personality disorder', results in the sufferer and their point of view becoming invalidated in relation to an authoritarian other. Unfortunately, embracing the seriously disturbed, the anxiety-provoking or the confused as equal partners in our attempts to understand ourselves or how best to respond to such problems is not easy because it challenges normative views of what we are. Distinctions between 'users' and 'providers' are shaped by the dynamics of the classic sick role, but both are victims of the need to sanitise and alienate distressing emotional distress as 'illness', rather than understand and study it for what it actually is.

## References

Alexander, J.W. (1985) 'The contributions of infection control to a century of surgical progress', *Annals of Surgery*, vol 201, no 4, pp 423–8.

Foucault, M. (2007 [1964]) *Madness and civilisation* (trans Howard, R.), Abingdon: Routledge Classics.

Gray, J.A.M. (1997) *Evidence-based health care*, Edinburgh: Churchill Livingstone.

Hope, J. (2009) 'Doctors want right to pray for patients without fear of reprisal', *Daily Mail*, 29 June. Available at: http://www.dailymail.co.uk/health/article-1196049/Doctors-want-right-pray-patients-fear-reprisal.html2009 (accessed 21 May 2012).

May, D. and Kelly, M.P. (1982) 'Chancers, pests and poor wee souls: problems of legitimation in psychiatric nursing', *Sociology of Health and Illness*, vol 4, no 3, pp 279–301.

Middleton, H. (2008) 'Whither DSM and ICD, Chapter V?', *Mental Health Review Journal*, vol 13, no 4, pp 4–15.

Moncrieff, J. (2008) *The myth of the chemical cure: A critique of psychiatric drug treatment*, Basingstoke: Palgrave Macmillan.

Parsons, T. (1951) *The social system*, London: Routledge & Kegan Paul.

Stiles, W.B., Barkham, M., Mellor-Cark, J. and Connell, J. (2008) 'Effectiveness of cognitive-behavioural, person-centred, and psychodynamic therapies in UK primary-care routine practice: replication in a larger sample', *Psychological Medicine*, vol 38, pp 77–88.

Williams, S.J. (2005) 'Parsons revisited: from the sick role to…?', *Health*, vol, 9, no 2, pp 123–44.

Worrall, J. (2010) 'Evidence: philosophy of science meets medicine', *Journal of Evaluation in Clinical Practice*, vol 16, no 2, pp 356–62.

# THREE

# Doing good carer-led research: reflecting on 'Past Caring' methodology

*Wendy Rickard and Rachel Purtell*

## Introduction

This chapter explores some key issues in doing service user-led research as well as you possibly think you can do it. It is about applying research theory. We aim to set out the methodological and practical details of a particular project we developed with a group of service users. In so doing, we explore how service user-led ideals can be translated into real-world research action, moving from theory to practice and from practice to theory. We aim to contribute to existing writing about the realities of collaboration in service user-led research, setting out how we pieced together a working method and how we were led by those we worked with. We use the recent Folk.us project titled 'Past Caring, a carer-led narrative research project about carer bereavement' as the case study example as it has current poignancy. Recent guidance suggested that 'The involvement of carers in research … is of real value. It has the potential to contribute to a culture in mental health where carers are respected, included and valued as key stakeholders within the mental health system' (Repper et al, 2012, p 28). We will not report here on the study outcomes relating to the phenomenon of carer bereavement, but rather focus on describing and reflecting on the development of better service user/carer-led research.

We asked the participant co-researchers in 'Past Caring' to reflect on their experience of doing this kind of carer-led, narrative research, and in this chapter, we also report what they said. We draw together participants' reflections from comments made and recorded at the end of their interviews, and from six-month feedback questionnaires. These are of interest within the wider context of mental health service users in research as they reveal people's real emotional and practical experiences of being part of a service user-led research initiative with a narrative focus and give people with mental health and other issues a voice in the debates. The wider project revealed that stress-related difficulties and breakdowns were the most central feature of people's overall bereavement challenges. Mental health issues were live in our research in terms of people's past lives and their range of bereavement experiences. Here, we recount their feelings about undertaking a very emotive, personal and revealing project like 'Past Caring' within this context. We particularly focus on the reported cathartic and capacity-building features of the research outcomes, stressing that this was a narrative research project with counselling support, not a therapeutic project in itself.

## Service user-led research

Three years ago, Folk.us was kick-starting a number of new projects as part of our brief to seek to give agency to service users, patients and carers to develop collaboratively their own research, which is as rigorous and credible as peer-reviewed research. Folk.us is part of the University of Exeter Medical School. Its main role is to support patients, service users and carers to design and undertake their own research across health or social care issues that are important to them. Folk.us staff take a small number of research ideas from patients, service users and carers' suggestions and work with them to develop these ideas into full, credible and rigorous research proposals. The aim is that the patient-, service user- and carer-led research proposals are presented to funders for consideration, and if successful in obtaining funding, Folk.us then continues to support the patients, service users and carers in working on the research projects.

Three local carers wanted to undertake some research on caring. Over five months, Folk.us helped them review literature and narrow ideas towards a project focus on carer bereavement. Together, we wanted to design a project where the participants were actively engaged in developing and planning the work, in the delivery of the work through their role as co-researchers and peer supporters, and in analysing the findings, writing up the project and disseminating the results to achieve a policy and service impact. This is an idealised version of the model put forward in *The DIY guide to survivor research* (Faulkner and Nicholls, 2002).

While we recognised that bereaved carers are a diverse group and have different lifestyles, abilities and needs, we also knew that they have a wealth of skills and experiences that could potentially be harnessed and enhanced to enrich their communities. We also wanted to be flexible in involving the people with more time and inclination more deeply, but also embracing those others who wanted involvement but not research responsibilities. Where specific new skills were needed in the project, we agreed to make skilled practitioners available to train the service users. With hindsight, this fitted well with Mike Oliver's emancipatory research model (Oliver, 1997) by:

- placing control in the hands of the researched, not the researcher;
- recognising that researchers have to learn how to put their knowledge and skills at the disposal of the research participants, for them to use in whatever ways they choose; and
- knowing that this was not about how to empower people (recognising that you cannot give people power), but once people have decided to empower themselves, exploring what research can do to facilitate this process.

Bereaved carers were defined as those with previous onerous caring duties who had to weave themselves a new kind of life when their cared-for person died, had dementia or left them for residential care. As such, we included people experiencing 'living bereavement'. The project was then built around bereaved carers coming together and inviting and enabling other bereaved carers to give their time, energy and skills within a user-led research project. We also aimed to provide bereaved carers with opportunities for social engagement and for building or enhancing peer networks through the research.

The project reflected values and principles that underpin the user movement more generally: empowerment; collective action in order to effect strategic and political change; partnership; and cooperation between service users. However, we recognise that, as Maddock et al (2004, p 1) suggest:

> although efforts are being made to consider the possibilities of user/survivor led research and the shift required to offer space to such a discourse in research, there are those in many corners who continue to resist them ... it is still an activity that sits on the fringes of user involvement.

By undertaking this project, we shared in a highly challenging but important goal to change the politics of research production (Beresford et al, 2008; Postle et al, 2008). Models for involving people in all levels of research in this way can be seen in a growing body of emancipatory research (Barnes, 2003; Beresford, 2002; Hanley, 2005), where shared authorship is key. We were helping to build on a growing body of partnership research in health and social care evident from the INVOLVE database. INVOLVE is a national advisory group that supports greater public involvement in NHS, public health and social care research. INVOLVE is funded by and part of the National Institute of Health Research (NIHR). Its role is to share knowledge and learning on public involvement in research.

## Research design

In order to offer the project originators the opportunity to learn new research methods and a research design that accommodated their existing research experiences, we chose a mixed-method, case study design, combining interviews with digital storytelling. Specific guidelines for the ethical conduct of research carried out by and with health service users were used (Faulkner, 2004; Hanley, 2005).

### Interviews

Semi-structured, one-to one, qualitative interviews were used (Kvale, 1996; Patton, 2002). Such interviews are considered useful to minimise potential threats experienced in relation to sensitive research topics (Lee, 1993). Participants were given the choice as to where they would prefer to do the interview, choosing between their own homes or an interviewing room in the University of Exeter Medical School. The interviews lasted for one to three hours. Our goal was to make sure that they were manageable and not too exhausting while allowing for in-depth and penetrating accounts to be revealed. An open-questioning technique was used, drawing on a question guide to broadly structure accounts.

For the interviews, we adopted what Bartunek and Louis (1996) describe as 'Insider/Outsider Team Research'. This model is informed by a stance that seeks to empower participants, combining in a research team people with varying degrees of cognitive, conceptual and social distance from the group to achieve a marginal perspective. 'Insider' researchers were two bereaved carers trained in interviewing techniques through Past Caring training workshops. Their tacit knowledge informed their interviewing (Griffith, 1998) and their 'insider' status was the entrée into the community of bereaved carers, 'offering greater possibilities for trust from participants' (Darlington and Scott, 2002, p 41). An 'insider' researcher will share cultural and personal understandings and may be better able to both empathise and to interrogate subtle nuances with an interviewee. An 'outsider' is someone with no intimate knowledge of the group being researched prior to her entry into the project team. Kvale suggests that the position of this interviewer should avoid and counteract risks described in the methodology literature as 'over-identification with participants ... maintaining a critical perspective on the knowledge gained' (Kvale, 1996, p 120) and particularly questioning 'assumed knowledge'. A Folk.us researcher acted as outsider. The informed choice of participants, within a feminist praxis, was our key guide as to who interviewed who (Darlington and Scott, 2002).

## Digital storytelling

Digital storytelling is a research technique that has become increasingly popular in recent years. It was introduced by the BBC to give television viewers and radio listeners a chance to make their own two-minute broadcast and publication on the internet. People were invited to workshops where they were taught technical and storytelling skills, script-writing and how to use industry standard image- and video-editing software. They made their own two-minute films or sound broadcasts. The experience of the BBC Telling Lives project was that the process had a natural integrity. The media often come in to a community, take stories away and deliver them back to people in a voice they do not recognise. However:

> Through this workshop process there is no mediator or professional producer editing the completed story ... participants deliver it to the producer in its finished form. There are no surprises for the storyteller when it is aired to the public. (Stephenson, 2008, p 3)

Digital stories are short (typically lasting two minutes), combining video, audio, still images and music that reveal patients' stories in a unique way. The method developed by Barrie Stephenson and his colleagues has taken many years to germinate and comes supported by a significant body of work (Meadows, 2003; Fyfe, 2007) and a manual and set of ethical guidelines for producing digital stories. The Past Caring workshops followed a set, practical programme where each individual created and produced their own digital story, using a collection of personal photographs, story circle techniques, script-writing, editing and film development, and working both in groups and individually.

## Participants

Previous qualitative studies of post-caring had used quite large samples and relatively short semi-structured interviews recorded at one sitting. Larkin interviewed 39 of an original sample of 44 (Larkin, 2009); Lewis and Meredith (1988) interviewed 41 former carers; McLaughlin and Ritchie (1994) interviewed 10; and Brown and Stetz (1999) interviewed 26 former carers. As a developmental study, Past Caring aimed to work more intensively with a smaller number of adult participants. It was a project of partnership with carers, who had agency and control in the project. As such, we were not conventionally sampling the population, but working in partnership with a purposefully small number of people to look at information-rich cases in depth and detail. This was one major jar with research convention. The Ethics Committee were worried about the validity of qualitative work with small numbers of participants, some of whom had got to know each other. We conceived it as snowball sampling, which is seen to be advantageous in this kind of sensitive context in that 'security' features are built into the method: 'Intermediaries who form the links of the referral chain are known to potential respondents and trusted by them. They are thus able to vouch for the researcher's *bona fides*' (Lee, 1993, p 67).

The participants were, initially, the three people who asked for Folk.us assistance to do the project. They had not previously worked together. They assembled a Research Advisory Group of seven people with an operational function to oversee the research team and to advise them on key areas (each had a strong track record in research involvement themselves). Together, they recommended other people who might like to participate and some community groups to approach. Prospective invitations were discussed. An element of 'theoretical sampling' was embraced in this process (Coyne, 1997). There are three main ways in which carers are often categorised (Twigg et al, 1990), in terms of features of:

- themselves (male carer, elderly carer);
- their dependants (carers of elderly people, carers of disabled children); and
- their relationships (spouse, parent, non-kin carers such as neighbours).

Often, research studies restrict themselves to one or other of these categories, but we openly invited individuals as a way to stress important parallels and contrasts between these 'service-oriented' groupings. We could not hope to be representative, but aimed for a mix of people relating to these categories, and some spread across our geographical area of Devon.

Most caring that people do is for two to three years, as a person ages and dies. However, for people with or who develop long-term disabilities, caring can be very long term or lifelong. Our focus was on the latter: people bereaved after a long-term caring experience (of up to 32 years). The age of our participants was limited to adults (aged 54 to 85 years old) – child and youth bereaved carers bring particular requirements for ethical permissions and procedures that we were not able to cater for. Our project did not allow for any systematic treatment of issues of class or race, in part due to our location in South Devon with its demographic of a predominantly white population. Our networking method meant that we engaged more with people who were mobile and those who had already had some contact with other carers. We also recognised that predominantly middle-class carers are likely to have greater access to resources, and this affected the caring experience and capacity for involvement in time-consuming research. The participants in this research project were paid research partners.

We recognise that bias was an almost inevitable feature of this sample, as of most others, 'because the social relations which underpin the sampling procedure tend towards reciprocity and transitivity.... Networks tend to turn in upon themselves and to be homogeneous in their attributes, rather than providing linkages to others whose social characteristics are different' (Lee, 1993, p 68). However, Patton (2002, p 563) suggests that in snowball sampling for small studies, 'the issue is not one of dealing with a distorted or biased sample, but rather one of clearly delineating the purpose and limitations of the sample studied'. In all, 11 people were invited to attend a project information afternoon and we spoke to eight other individuals during the course of the project who had expressed interest. Eight participants decided to take part and were available for the negotiated workshop dates.

Reflexivity was an essential part of this participative method. There was discussion and reflection within the project advisory group of transparent, sensitive and non-coercive recruitment, leaving an audit trail of decisions made, clearly reporting any refusals and monitoring the impact on method and conclusions. People who chose not to take part were not required to give their reasons. However, those that volunteered information said that the timing (when the sessions ran) and the overall time commitment (especially for the digital story-making) were too onerous. Some were balancing other caring roles (particularly for grandchildren and living partners). Some booked holidays and other activities at short notice and had to drop out. A few were suspicious of the project goals, being concerned that the products would be amateurish and unconvincing.

## Participant reflections

Overall, each participant said that they valued the 'Past Caring' project experience, with general comments like: "but personally it's been good for me" (Brian); "yeah, I think it's been good" (Gill); and "it was of great benefit" (John). For everyone, it was an emotional experience, and because of the sadness of bereavement, not necessarily easy. Liz said: "that's been fine [telling the story]". Susan said it was "quite uncomfortable ... but very good ... it's been very positive, all right, and ... [crying] I find talking about Tom's death still difficult". Brian mentioned the way that it had taken him back to emotions he had experienced earlier in his bereavement, saying: "it reignites feelings and emotions that I thought I'd got over". Rosemary said: "It's felt okay. It's brought back lots of sad memories. I've cried a lot. But it's all right. Yeah. It's okay ... I mean, I haven't minded." And Kath reported: "It's been fine.... A number of emotional issues that had been well buttoned down were surfaced by this process. This had both negative and positive effects: increasing stress and anxiety but enabling reflection and positive action."

Using terms like 'it's been fine' and 'I haven't minded' expresses some reservation about voicing difficult and often traumatic experiences. There are resonances here with work that has been done with Holocaust survivors and in other traumatic and taboo-laden situations (Rickard, 1998; Rouverall et al, 2000). There are aspects of revealing difficult stories that are uncomfortable and uneasy. Both Kath and others, however, went on to emphasise the value of putting the stories somewhere, of taking stock and reorienting themselves for the future, almost in properly acknowledging and re-evaluating what they had been (and were still going) through. Kath said:

> "I think it's really useful for me to make time to remember the journey. It's painful, but as I said off-tape, it's actually painful whether I talk about it or not, and actually bringing it to the surface and looking at it now and again I think is something that's quite useful to do.... I went to a lecture by a sociologist called Erik Olin Wright and he talked about us trying to create a better world and it being like a journey, and he said that every now and again you have to climb one of the tallest trees and look at where you've been, and

are you still headed in the direction where you want to
go? And I think that's, for me, what, what this is all about."

Rosemary said: "I think it's quite cathartic, actually, talking through
these things". Victoria similarly commented: "I just think making the
digi-story was a good thing for me personally ... because for me it's
processing what's happened, and it's also, in that you learn more things
about it as you process it". Participants were able to explore the wider
context of bereavement in their lives as a whole through the project.
Liz was very worried about telling her story at the outset, but, on
reflection, felt that the telling helped her to recognise a 'residual guilt'
that needed putting "in the right place":

> "And I, I'd hope that people would think that they should
> be able to challenge and should be able to ask questions
> and not be intimidated, and stick it out. But I think you
> also probably have to recognise that you're likely to still be
> left with some guilt, 'Did I do enough? Should I have done
> this, should I have done that, did I handle that properly?'
> And I think that's going to go on, for me, for years, really,
> because I have these moments when I think, 'Why didn't I
> do that? What about that?' And, you know, there's nothing
> I can do about it now. Have to live with it, I suppose, and
> put it in the right place."

Liz used the project to reorient her memories towards her husband:

> "Having listened to the digi-story, I realised that I had not
> shared enough about how I admired my husband's ability
> to cope quietly and largely positively with his failing health
> and shrinking life. Perhaps I needed to get the very negative
> and emotionally hard things about his treatment in hospital
> out of the way to be able to move on. This I think I may
> have achieved as a result of sharing it with people who have
> been there as well."

Gill said: "The interview gave me a chance to reflect on my relationship
with my parents. I did not grieve for them but it was obvious that
I needed to reflect on my life after their demise." Participants noted
subtle differences in how they felt depending on the time since
their bereavement. For some, bereavement was relatively recent and
still rather raw, but even those who had been bereaved many years

previously, like Kath, whose son, Sam, had died 11 years ago, felt that there was value in refocusing on the bereavement experience through the project. When asked who she would most like to hear her story, Kath said: "Me! [Laughing.] It is about reminding me of the journey." This perhaps highlights the long shadow that bereavement casts: that bereavement does not finish one day, but is something that changes life for the bereaved carer long into the future and is usefully revisited at times. This suggests that in line with other research on life review and reminiscence, telling bereavement stories is personal and intense and a particularly powerful, active way to rehearse and 'retrospectively mediate' or come to terms with the past (Bennett and Vidal-Hall, 2000). Kath went on to say:

> "I can't really begin to describe the impact of being involved in this project. Looking for photographs led me to open drawers and albums that I had not looked into for years. Some of this was very confronting and distressing. However, it has led me to move forward in a number of areas, sorting and clearing and reconnecting with people I had lost touch with."

For Victoria, whose experience of living bereavement was ongoing at the time the project was being written up, the rawness of the bereavement was a huge issue. Victoria later said:

> "It took a long time for the project to get funding and when the introductory day came, I went home thinking maybe I didn't want to be involved – I felt a long way from N's diagnosis in 2004 and I wasn't sure I wanted to face that raw grief again. I am so glad that I continued with the project."

Participants noted how their confidence had fluctuated during the course of the project. Recruiting participants to take part was complex. We know that some people were put off taking part because they did not want to 'come out' as a carer – they resisted acknowledging that identity and to take part, people were essentially forced to. Several of the people who initially liked the idea of the project said that they had felt slightly uncomfortable before coming to the first session. Gill said: "I must admit that I went in with fear and trepidation; the very confident person who is actually in fear and trepidation of all the technical stuff". Brian said: "I greatly enjoyed [it] and I'm glad I was included 'cos initially I was going to opt out to allow someone else to do it, but I'm glad that I did it". John said: "It did help my confidence … I shall certainly make use of what I learned in making it [the digistory]". Victoria, who also became a co-trainer, went further and said: "It has restored the identity and confidence I lost when I left work through stress, and enabled me to use skills I thought were lost to me, as well as learning new ones".

Bennett and Vidal-Hall (2000, p 423) suggest that narrative work around death allows people to define their past identity as wife, nurse, organiser, carer, worker and their present identity as 'chief mourner'. Victoria is perhaps hinting that adding new skills aided her in piecing together a future identity too.

The stories also seemed to help people get their version of events validated by others. Victoria said: "It felt safe for me to acknowledge my grief in the group. We were all there because of our loss." This point about sharing bereavement experiences within the group was key. Liz said: "I enjoyed participating in the project and learnt a lot about other people's experiences and coping skills". Liz felt that the project came to her at an important moment in her post-bereavement re-engagement with the world:

> "I think bereavement is overlooked by professionals, unless you need a pill. But it has a profound effect for a long time, whether it is unexpected due to an accident or sudden death or longer term as with dementia or a deteriorating condition. Long-term carers particularly have issues that persist sometimes for the rest of their lives unless something is done to re-engage them meaningfully in life."

Other researchers have written about the value of an opportunity to 'tell it like it is', of a need to 'make sense of it all', and by 'offering experiences up', bereaved people implicitly invite others to help create meaning and to negotiate an acceptable version of events (Bennett and Vidal-Hall, 2000, p 424). Recent research has highlighted that practical, ethical, methodological and emotional challenges are experienced by those conducting research around death and bereavement (Kendall et al, 2007). We feel that we succeeded in giving bereaved carers an unmediated voice. Having that voice was not easy for them and the reflections reveal strongly that no one came lightly to this project.

We suggest that the project case study design, using sound interviews and digital stories worked and was very enthusiastically received, though no one participating had familiarity with the methods at the outset. We feel that excellent carer involvement was achieved, with carers initiating the project and taking control of the research design, implementation and dissemination. In this sense, we did make opportunities for and remove barriers to carers doing their own research and we did raise the profile of carers within the care system. Some participants found the time commitment of the analysis, write-up and dissemination activities very onerous (because it is!) and it was interesting how the input from different team members meant that they were able to commit more or less at different times (not reported here). It was central that we had research support from a small and intensely personal agency like Folk.us. We wonder what will happen now that the research development and involvement work that such small groups once undertook has been mainstreamed in wide-scale, nationally driven public participation initiatives.

## References

Barnes, C. (2003) 'What a difference a decade makes: reflections on a decade of doing "emancipatory" disability research', *Disability & Society*, vol 18, no 1, pp 3–17.

Bartunek, J.M. and Louis, M.R. (1996) *Insider/outsider team research*, London: Sage.

Bennett, KM. and Vidal-Hall, S. (2000) 'Narratives of death: a qualitative study of widowhood in later life', *Ageing and Society*, vol 20, pp 413–28.

Beresford, P. (2002) 'User involvement in research and evaluation: liberation or regulation?', *Social Policy and Society*, vol 1, no 2, pp 95–105.

Beresford, P., Croft, S. and Adshead, L. (2008) '"We don't see her as a social worker": a service user case study of the importance of the social worker's relationship and humanity', *British Journal of Social Work*, vol 38, no 7, pp 1388–407.

Brown, M. and Stetz, K. (1999) 'The labour of caregiving: a theoretical model of care-giving during potentially fatal illness', *Qualitative Health Research*, vol 9, no 2, pp 182–97.

Coyne, I. (1997) 'Sampling in qualitative research. Purposeful and theoretical sampling: merging or clear boundaries?', *Journal of Advanced Nursing*, vol 26, pp 623–30.

Darlington, Y. and Scott, D. (2002) *Qualitative research in practice: stories from the field*, Buckingham: Open University Press.

Faulkner, A. (2004) *The ethics of survivor research: guidelines for the ethical conduct of research carried out by mental health service users and survivors*, London: Joseph Rowntree Foundation.

Faulkner, A. and Nicholls, V. (2002) *The DIY guide to survivor research: everything you always wanted to know about survivor-led research but were afraid to ask*, London: The Mental Health Foundation.

Fyfe, H. (2007) '"Habits of the heart": storytelling and everyday life', seminar paper presented at the George Ewart Evans Centre for Storytelling, the University of Glamorgan, 14 June.

Griffith, A.I. (1998) 'Insider/outsider: epistemological privilege and mothering work', *Human Studies*, vol 21, no 4, pp 361–76.

Hanley, B. (2005) *Research as empowerment? Report of a series of seminars organised by the Toronto Group*, London: Joseph Rowntree Foundation.

Kendall, M., Harris, F., Boyd, K., Sheikh, A., Murray, S.A., Brown, D., Mallinson, I., Kearney, N. and Worth, A. (2007) 'Key challenges and ways forward in researching the "good death": qualitative in-depth interview and focus group study', *British Medical Journal*, Online First, doi:10.1136/bmj.39097.582639.55 (28 Feb).

Kvale, S. (1996) *InterViews, an introduction to qualitative research interviewing*, London: Sage.

Larkin, M. (2009) 'Life after caring: the post caring experiences of former carers', *British Journal of Social Work*, vol 39, pp 1026–42.

Lee, R. (1993) *Doing research on sensitive topics*, London: Sage.

Lewis, J. and Meredith, B. (1988) *Daughters who care*, London: Routledge.

Maddock, J., Lineham, D., Shears, J. and ASSURT (Action by Survivors/Service Users Research Team) (2004) 'Empowering mental health research: user led research into the care programme approach', *Research Policy and Planning*, vol 22, no 2, p 29. Available at: http://www.ssrg.org.uk/publications/rpp/2004/issue2/article5.pdf

McLaughlin, E. and Ritchie, J. (1994) 'Legacies of caring: the experiences and circumstances of ex-carers', *Health and Social Care*, vol 2, no 4, pp 241–53.

Meadows, D. (2003) 'Digital storytelling – research-based practice in new media', *Visual Communication*, vol 2, no 2, pp 189–93.

Oliver, M. (1997) 'Emancipatory research: realistic goal or impossible dream?', in C. Barnes and G. Mercer (eds) *Doing disability research*, Leeds: The Disability Press, pp 15–31.

Patton, M.Q. (2002) *Qualitative research and evaluation methods* (3rd edn), London: Sage.

Postle, K., Beresford, P. and Hardy, S. (2008) 'Assessing research and involving people in using health and social care services: addressing the tensions', *Evidence and Policy*, vol 4, no 3, pp 251–62.

Repper, J., Simpson, A. and Grimshaw, G. (2012) *Good practice guidance for involving carers, family members and close friends of service users in research*, London: Mental Health Research Network.

Rickard, W. (1998) 'Oral history – more dangerous than therapy?', *Oral History*, vol 26, no 20, pp 34–48.

Rouverall, A., Kerr, D., Rickard, W. and Thomson, A. (2000) 'Shaping and rehearsing a chronic illness oral history', Panel on Shared Authority, International Oral History Association Conference Proceedings, Istanbul, Turkey, 15–19 June.

Stephenson, B. (2008) 'Storytelling with BBC Telling Lives'. Available at: http://www.digistories.co.uk/about.htm

Twigg, J., Atkin, K. and Perring, C. (1990) *Carers and services: a review of research*, London: Social Policy Research Unit/HMSO.

## FOUR

# Theorising service user involvement from a researcher perspective

*Katherine C. Pollard and David Evans*

## Introduction

There has been a growing momentum concerning patient and public involvement (PPI) in research over the last decade in the UK, with the concomitant establishment of appropriate infrastructure, in particular, the development of INVOLVE (Hanley et al, 2004), which is supported by the Department of Health (DH) expressly to promote PPI in research. In 2005, the DH explicitly stated that members of the public, including service users (patients) and carers, should be actively involved in 'design, conduct, analysis and reporting of research' (DH, 2005), while the National Institute for Health Research (NIHR) increasingly requires evidence of active public involvement when commissioning health care research (NIHR, 2012). The NIHR is one of two main public bodies (the other being the Medical Research Council) through which health care research is funded in the UK, and is therefore hugely influential in this area. Principles for good practice when involving service users in research have also been published in different areas of health care, in particular mental health (UK Mental Health Research Network, 2011).

Over a similar period, theorists and other academics have started to develop and codify knowledge concerning issues arising from PPI in research. These have included the definition of different models of participation and a discussion of different conceptions of knowledge itself (Nolan et al, 2007; Oliver et al, 2008; Morrow et al, 2010). In this chapter, we intend to discuss some of these issues in relation to our real-world experience of leading and working on academic-funded projects in which service users have played active roles to varying extents.

At the University of the West of England (UWE), over the last five years, we have had a particular focus on working with service users across a range of activities within the institution, including research. We have assigned the term 'service user research partner' to those individuals, neither academics nor health or social care practitioners, who have been active within research projects. In 2010, we produced a guide for good practice for involving service users in research, developed jointly by services users, carers, academics, practitioners and members of the public (UWE, 2010). In this chapter, we will refer to 'service user researchers' to denote service users, carers or members of the public who are actively involved in research projects, and to 'researchers' to denote academic or clinical researchers.

Some of our service user research partners have been or are users of mental health services, and some of our projects have been located within the area of mental health. However, many of our service user research partners and research projects have been situated within other areas of health and social care. Our experience across all these projects has led us to recognise that there are issues arising from PPI in research that are unrelated to the area of care or service delivery; it is from this recognition that we approach our task of theorising service user involvement from a researcher perspective.

It should be noted that care for mental health is unlike other health care areas in the UK as it is the only area where service users can be treated without their consent, a course of action enshrined in law since the early 1840s (Fennel, 1996). There has consequently been a relatively high and long-standing degree of activism among mental health service users (Crossley, 1999), accompanied by a drive for PPI in service design, delivery and research. Researchers in this area, therefore, have a longer history of considering and engaging with PPI in research than researchers in many other areas of health and social care. By contrast, in our experience, professionals in some other areas of health care and research are still not aware of PPI, despite recent developments and the growing literature.

## Researcher attitudes to PPI

An important starting place is to ask what we already know about researchers' attitudes to PPI in research, both generally and in terms of attitudes in mental health research. There is an emerging evidence base on the impact of PPI on research, which has been collated and synthesised in two recent literature reviews (Staley, 2009; Brett et al, 2010). Both reviews consider the impact of PPI, which gives some insights into researchers' attitudes. The reviews found that PPI has been reported to have both positive and negative impacts on researchers.

Positive impacts included: increased enjoyment and satisfaction from working in partnership with the public; career benefits; and, most relevant to this discussion, positive challenges to their beliefs and attitudes (Hewlett et al, 2006). One team of mental health service researchers reported:

> Having a service user as part of the team made other team members try to consider how users would think and feel in mental health services and when reading our report. It made us challenge our own assumptions, consider our language and to be very honest and open with ourselves about our attitudes and values. (Clark et al, 2004, p 34)

However, researchers have also reported that involving the public often requires significant time, energy and/or financial resources, which can lead to frustration on their part. Some researchers are sceptical about the value of PPI or have negative attitudes because of what they regard as negative previous experiences of involvement. Researchers may also find it difficult to relinquish control or share power in research (Brett et al, 2010).

There have been a number of articles about PPI in research in which researchers already committed to involvement demonstrate their positive attitudes towards it (eg Hewlett et al, 2006; Staniszewska et al, 2007). There are, of course, a number of service user researchers, particularly in mental health, who unsurprisingly express very positive attitudes towards PPI in research (Rose, 2004; Beresford, 2007). We have much less concrete information about researchers who are sceptical or hostile towards PPI in research (for they do not tend to write articles about it), although stories of such attitudes are commonly recounted by the advocates of involvement. There have been relatively few research studies specifically on researchers' attitudes towards PPI in research. The most significant contribution in this area has been the two papers by a team of researchers mainly based in Sheffield, who undertook a study specifically on health researchers' attitudes towards involving the public in research (Thompson et al, 2009; Ward et al, 2010). They conducted a qualitative study with 15 purposively sampled UK-based university health researchers and found a mixed picture of positive beliefs in the benefits of involving the public alongside some feelings of apprehension and discomfort.

Although based on a small sample, this mixed picture of researchers' attitudes towards involvement is consistent with the literature discussed earlier and our own experiences. In particular, Ward et al (2009) identify the issues of 'epistemological dissonance' (a lack of recognition that service users can bring valid forms of knowledge to bear on research) and the 'know–do gap' (between researchers' stated belief in the value of PPI and their actual practices). They link these issues to researchers' professionalisation strategies for privileging their 'expert' knowledge over service users' lay knowledge based on lived experience, thus maintaining their power and status as researchers relative to service users. However strong our personal commitments to PPI and however good our relationships with service users, as academic researchers, we have to acknowledge and reflect upon these power–knowledge dynamics, which inevitably shape our relationships with service users in research, whether we are conscious of them or not.

## Implications of PPI for research and researchers

Much has been written about the benefits accruing to service users and members of the public when authentic PPI occurs in research projects (eg Faulkner, 2009; Lowes et al, 2011). There is also evidence which suggests that PPI enhances the quality of research (Faulkner, 2009; Staley, 2009; Lowes et al, 2011). The need to establish whether this is the case or not, and to determine what conditions are necessary for a favourable outcome in this regard, has resulted in the NIHR funding three projects and the Medical Research Council one, all ongoing at the time of writing, to measure the impact of PPI in research. However, as stated earlier, relatively little has been written about the researcher experience in the context of PPI.

It is a truism to state that research needs researchers; equally, researchers need research. For many researchers, a lack of funded projects can mean lack of employment and even the end of a career. These researchers must, therefore, keep abreast of, and comply with, changing imperatives in conducting research in order to remain employed. The necessity for gaining ethical approval is an example of such an imperative; surprising though it may seem, it is only relatively recently that ethical review became mandatory for research projects within health care (DH, 2001). Similarly, researchers applying for many funding schemes must now engage with PPI in their projects. It is important to recognise this element of compulsion in the current context; while most service users and carers who become actively engaged in research do so from conviction and a passionate wish to have their voice heard, it cannot be assumed that all researchers are equally passionate about PPI in research. While there are undoubtedly many who have a strong commitment to providing opportunities for the service user voice to be heard, it should also be recognised that there are considerable numbers of jobbing researchers for whom PPI is merely one imperative among many others with which they must comply. This situation can be compounded by a researcher's academic discipline, which may focus entirely on a research paradigm that is not necessarily easily aligned with PPI principles.

## Theoretical framing for research

There are differing perspectives and differing paradigms of research, and PPI fits more easily into some than others. Different research paradigms can be conceptualised along a continuum, with approaches grounded in positivistic enquiry (eg randomised controlled trials) at one end, and those recognising the shifting complexity of the self and of social situations (eg participatory enquiry) at the other (Guba and Lincoln, 1994; Heron and Reason, 1997). Unsurprisingly, PPI in research has grown from approaches such as participatory enquiry (Nolan et al, 2007). It is fairly obvious that PPI can easily be incorporated into an approach that values, even demands, an active contribution from all those involved (Heron and Reason, 1997). For example, in participatory and many qualitative approaches, with appropriate support, service users can be involved in all the research processes, including study design and collection and analysis of data (Hopper and Lincoln, 2009; Moule et al, 2011). In these approaches, it is also possible to adopt a relatively flexible attitude to the conceptualisation and construction of knowledge, since any assumption that knowledge is necessarily objective and value-free is itself called into question (Nolan et al, 2007). It therefore becomes congruent to accord value to 'situated' knowledge, that is, knowledge that does not derive from professional or academic sources.

It is more difficult to incorporate more participatory types of PPI into positivistic research approaches. Although service users can certainly be involved in framing research questions, identifying outcomes relevant to service users and selecting study instruments (Campbell, 2009; Del vecchio and Blyler, 2009; Edwards et al, 2011), the data collection and processing methods employed often require specialised knowledge and skills. It is generally unrealistic to expect service users to acquire these skills, or to expect researchers to involve service users without the prerequisite skills actively in these processes. In addition, positivistic enquiry assumes that 'real' knowledge is objective and derived from measurable sources, which is the domain of professional or academic 'experts'; this assumption results in subjective experience, such as the service user voice, being accorded relatively less value or compartmentalised to only specific parts of the research process.

Despite increasing recognition of the validity and usefulness of a range of different research paradigms, the belief persists in some circles that results of research from positivistic enquiry, assumed to be neutral and objective, and underpinned by statistical theory, are intrinsically of more value than those derived from 'softer' approaches, such as participatory enquiry. That this is the case in health care research is evidenced by the format of application forms for research funding and for ethical review, many of which still ask direct questions about the statistical and scientific methods to be employed, regardless of which research approach has been chosen. Given the comparative limitations of organising PPI in positivistic enquiry, this inherent bias in its favour in practice mitigates against service user involvement in the conduct of a large body of health care research, other than within narrowly defined and limited parameters, such as at the design stage or assisting in dissemination.

## Power issues

As has been mentioned in various chapters in this volume, the exercise of power in research incorporating PPI is an obvious issue for consideration. There is no doubt that unequal power relationships can have a major effect on the quality and extent of PPI in a project. Extreme cases of power imbalances can result in only tokenistic PPI, where service users are not given genuine opportunities for active involvement in a project, but are included simply as 'window dressing'. However, there has been little recognition of the way that power issues in PPI research can also affect researchers negatively. As stated earlier, service user researchers usually want to be involved in research projects due to their own strong feelings about the area of care, arising from personal experience, or the experience of someone close to them. In our experience, it can therefore be quite disappointing for them to discover how long research findings can take to get into the public domain, and also that there is no guarantee, and, in fact, often little likelihood, that findings from a project will be implemented in a service area.

Barriers to implementation of research findings in practice have been well documented (eg Mantzoukas, 2008; Greenhalgh and Russell, 2009). Service users often do not realise that many, if not most, researchers are powerless in this area. Consequently, researchers working on PPI projects often have to engage in considerable emotional work in order to support service users to manage the disappointment arising from the realisation of the reality of the relationship between research and practice in health and social care. As it is common for funded research projects to be conducted with barely adequate time and resources, and with the deadlines and demands of funders to meet, this emotional work can add considerably to the stress experienced by researchers who are responsible for ensuring that a project is conducted to sufficiently high academic standards within the time specified.

## Skills

Any individual involved actively in a research project must have the skills required to fulfil their role. In a PPI project, researchers must ensure that this is the case for all the service user researchers. When researchers are recruited to work on a project, it is common for them to have to provide a curriculum vitae that details their research skills and experience. While service user researchers may be asked to provide similar information before being invited to a project, there is often a process of negotiation that needs to be completed in order to ensure that they are equipped for particular research tasks.

The senior researchers in the project first need to ascertain to what extent service user researchers wish to be involved; this can range along a continuum from providing advice on particular topics to undertaking a variety of research tasks, including data collection and analysis and contributing to writing project reports. Training for service user researchers in particular aspects of research often needs to be arranged externally, or provided within the project, in order to enable them to function adequately. Allowing this level of flexibility, if possible, is important to allow service user researchers to grow as researchers. In turn, this can be beneficial for current and future projects. However, it should be remembered that not all service user researchers want to develop involvement in research. In particular, some service user researchers may feel overwhelmed by perceived expectations concerning their own skills, performance and responsibility (Shields et al, 2007). Researchers need to be sensitive to this situation, and may have to depart from the agreed allocation of tasks within the project as it progresses in order to support the service user researchers. This process obviously requires that researchers have sufficient sensitivity, and are able to communicate with the service user researchers about these issues. They also need to be able to negotiate satisfactory ways forward, and be prepared to increase their own task commitments in order to facilitate the service user researchers' input into the project.

## Running a project

Even for researchers, such as ourselves, who are strongly committed to involving the public in research, there often remain fundamental tensions between including members of the public fully in research and having to deliver the research outputs and outcomes required by funders and employing institutions. The benefits are increasingly recognised in the literature (Staley, 2009; Brett et al, 2010), but it is also important to reflect on the costs, particularly the emotional costs and tensions, which are not often discussed. Often, the catalyst for these is the conflicting pull between the efficiency/quality drives (getting the research done to the necessary standards for funders and academic publication) and the empowerment agenda (giving service users a real voice in decision-making). National policy and the literature imply that the two drives are complementary, but, in our experience, they often conflict, and this can lead to emotional work for the researcher, who has to try to find a compromise that balances the competing drives. Similarly, researchers often have to balance and mediate between service users' individual needs (both practical and emotional) and often inflexible institutional policy, procedures and practices. In the best-case scenario, where the research is well funded, there may be a PPI coordinator or administrator who will take some of the pressure off the researcher and sort out the practicalities. Often, however, it will be the principal investigator or another researcher in the team who has to take responsibility for managing this tension.

A key question, particularly relevant when working with service users with long-term conditions, is how you deal with illness, particularly episodic illness which means that as a researcher, you can never be sure when a service user will be in a position to contribute. This is less an issue when they are one of several individuals contributing in an advisory capacity, but becomes more intense when they are a core member of the research team and may have significant responsibilities, including data collection and processing. This raises a fundamental issue about the nature of the 'contract' between the university, the researcher and the service user. Assuming, as is good practice, and as our institution does, that service users are paid for their time, do you agree a formal contract with them, and, if so, how do you contract for potential episodic illness? Our approach has been to avoid formal contracts and pay for hours worked on a 'casual claim' basis. This allows the service user some flexibility to balance their work and illness, and avoids committing all the institutional resources where the work may not materialise, but it does mean the potential casualisation of the service user contribution. Moreover, if a service user is ill long term, it still leaves the researcher with a conundrum of whether to wait for their health to improve (with possible deadlines looming) or seek to involve a 'replacement' service user. In our experience, it is best to broach the possibility of a service user having to withdraw completely from a study, and to negotiate and plan for this eventuality at the start of a project.

There is often a large amount of emotional work for the researcher in these situations, both in terms of seeking to support the service users and in managing institutional policies and practices into which the service user researcher does not easily fit. As a member of staff, you are often the face of the institution to the service user, and therefore may be the recipient of their frustration (and sometimes anger) at non-service user-friendly institutional systems and practices. Many of these frustrations and tensions relate to payment and expenses issues, where university finance departments do not have a service user category of employment. As researchers, we sometimes need to do things 'under the radar', adapting and reinterpreting university procedures. Such work can be time-consuming and frustrating, and the researcher is never quite sure when she or he may be 'caught out' and criticised for bending the bureaucratic rules. Often, this emotional work is equally hidden from institutional managers and service user researchers. Similarly, negotiating service users' access to NHS Trusts as researchers can prove lengthy and difficult, as Trust processes are not generally structured to allow for service users in that capacity.

A final area of emotional work can be managing meetings with service users. Researchers and service users may have a common interest in research projects succeeding, but they often come with very different assumptions, aims and world views, which may be difficult to integrate (del Vecchio and Blyler, 2009). Sometimes, as researchers, we can find it very frustrating when from our perspectives, service users digress wildly from the agenda, but we feel inhibited to challenge them directly in the same way that we would an academic colleague. There are complex power issues in the relationship between researchers and service user researchers, but, as mentioned earlier, not all the power is exercised by the former; the authority to speak as a service user and dominate proceedings is a potent power for some service user researchers. In these situations, particularly when deadlines draw near, the temptation for researchers can be to take the line of least resistance to produce work that will sufficiently satisfy both the funders and the service user researchers. This can result in researchers producing outputs with which they themselves are not satisfied, as they have prioritised the lack of tension in the research team and delivery to deadlines above academic considerations.

From the preceding, it should be evident that even when you are genuinely committed to fully involving service users in a project, it can be hard always to do so well in practice. Deadlines are tight, and academic colleagues are often on hand for corridor conversations, or at least they are likely to be checking emails regularly, sometimes late at night or at weekends, when service users are less likely to be available online. With the best will in the world, you cannot always manage to keep service user researchers equally in the loop with academic colleagues, and you then face the additional emotional work of the guilt that you are not living up to your own values. This emotional work for researchers in involving service users needs to be weighed in the balance alongside the 'epistemological dissonance' and professionalising strategies to maintain researchers' power and status, identified by Ward et al (2009), in order to come to a more nuanced understanding of the different drivers and challenges facing researchers in this area.

However, whatever problems occur, when a project has been completed satisfactorily, it is often the case that a positive relationship has developed between all those involved. At this point, service user researchers may be keen to get involved in other research, particularly where they have acquired particular skills sets that they wish to maintain or develop further. In this situation, researchers may have to consider how to support the service users in subsequent activities. It can be argued that having invited service users into a project, which has subsequently benefited from their particular perspective and their acquired skills, researchers have a moral imperative to be involved to some extent in their further development. Where researchers acknowledge and accept this responsibility, there are obviously further time and resource implications for them that they then need to manage.

## Conclusion

PPI in research, while of undoubted merit and productive of benefit to researchers and service users, is actually more difficult and problematic to manage in the real world than discussion in the guidance and most of the literature implies; it is a classic case of dissonance between theory and practice. Researchers tend to report the positive aspects of PPI, and not the difficulties and emotional work. Academic, clinical and service user researchers need to create space for reflection on, and honest dialogue about, these 'wicked issues' within research projects and programmes, and the research community as a whole needs to reflect more honestly on this if PPI in research policy and practice is to advance. In particular, bureaucratic academic and care systems and the expectations of both researchers and service user researchers need to be managed effectively so that projects are not hampered by conflicting perspectives, frustrating red tape and unrealistic goals, but rather enhanced by the inclusion of diversity and the acceptance of individuals' differing degrees of engagement, capacities and skills sets.

## References

Barnes, C. (1992) 'Qualitative research: valuable or irrelevant?', *Disability, Handicap and Society*, vol 7, no 2, pp 115–24.

Beresford, P. (2007) 'The role of service user research in generating knowledge-based health and social care: from conflict to contribution', *Evidence & Policy*, vol 3, no 3, pp 329–41.

Bochner, A. (1994) 'Perspectives on inquiry II: theories and stories', in M. Knapp and G. Miller (eds) *Handbook of interpersonal communication*, Thousand Oaks, CA: Sage, pp 21–41.

Brett, J., Staniszewska, S., Mockford, C., Seers, K., Herron-Marx, S. and Baylis, H. (2010) *The PIRICON study: a systematic review of the conceptualization, measurement, impact and outcomes of patient and public involvement in health and social care research*, London: UKCRC.

Campbell, J. (2009) 'Methods', in J. Wallcraft, B. Schrank and M. Amering (eds) *Handbook of service user involvement in mental health research*, Chichester: Wiley-Blackwell, pp 113–37.

Clark, M., Glasby, J. and Lester, H. (2004) 'Cases for change: user involvement in mental health services and research', *Research Policy & Planning*, vol 22, no 2, pp 31–8.

Crossley, N. (1999) 'Fish, field, habitus and madness: the first wave mental health users movement in Great Britain', *The British Journal of Sociology*, vol 50, no 4, pp 647–70.

del Vecchio, P. and Blyler, C.R. (2009) 'Topics', in J. Wallcraft, B. Schrank and M. Amering (eds) *Handbook of service user involvement in mental health research*, Chichester: Wiley-Blackwell, pp 99–112.

DH (Department of Health) (2001) *Research governance framework for health and social care*, London: Department of Health.

DH (2005) *Best research for best health: a national health research strategy. The NHS contribution to health research in England: a consultation*, London: Department of Health.

Edwards, V., Wyatt, K. and Logan, S. (2011) 'Consulting parents about the design of a randomized controlled trial of osteopathy for children with cerebral palsy', *Health Expectations*, vol, no 4, pp 429–38.

Ellis, C. and Bochner, A. (2000) 'Autoethnography, personal narrative, reflexivity', in N. Denzin and Y. Lincoln (eds) *Handbook of qualitative research* (2nd edn), Thousand Oaks, CA: Sage, pp 733–68.

Faulkner, A. (2009) 'Principles and motives', in J. Wallcraft, B. Schrank and M. Amering (eds) *Handbook of service user involvement in mental health research*, Chichester: Wiley-Blackwell, pp 13–24.

Fennel, P. (1996) *Treatment without consent: law, psychiatry and the treatment of mentally disordered people since 1845*, London: Routledge.

Greenhalgh, T. and Russell, J. (2009) 'Evidence-based policy making: a critique', *Perspectives in Biology and Medicine*, vol 52, no 2, pp 304–18.

Guba, E.G. and Lincoln, Y.S. (1994) 'Competing paradigms in qualitative research', in N.K. Denzin and Y.S. Lincoln (eds) *Handbook of qualitative research*, Thousand Oaks, CA: Sage.

Hanley, B., Bradburn, J., Barnes, M. et al (2004) *Involving the public in NHS, public health and social care research: briefing notes for researchers* (2nd edn), Eastleigh: INVOLVE.

Heron, J. and Reason, P. (1997) 'A participatory inquiry paradigm', *Qualitative Inquiry*, vol 3, no 3, pp 274–94.

Hewlett, S., de Wit, M., Richards, P., Quest, E., Hughes, R., Heiberg, T. and Kirwan, J. (2006) 'Patients and professionals as research partners: challenges, practicalities and benefits', *Arthritis and Rheumatism*, vol 55, no 4, pp 676–80.

Hopper, K. and Lincoln, A. (2009) 'Capacity-building', in J. Wallcraft, B. Schrank and M. Amering (eds) *Handbook of service user involvement in mental health research*, Chichester: Wiley-Blackwell, pp 73–86.

Lowes, L., Robling, M.R., Bennert, K., Crawley, C., Hambly, H., Hawthorne, K. and Gregory, J.W. (2011) 'Involving lay and professional stakeholders in the development of a research intervention for the DEPICTED study', *Health Expectations*, vol 14, no 3, pp 250–60.

Mantzoukas, S. (2008) 'A review of evidence-based practice, nursing research and reflection: levelling the hierarchy', *Journal of Clinical Nursing*, vol 17, no 2, pp 214–23.

Morrow, E., Ross, F., Grocott, P. and Bennett, J. (2010) 'A model and measure for quality service user involvement in health research', *International Journal of Consumer Studies*, vol 34, no 5, pp 532–9.

Moule, P., Young, P., Albarran, J., Oliver, B., Curran, T., Hopkinson, C., Pollard, K., Hadfield, J., Lima, M. and Rice, C. (2011) *Leadership course evaluation with patient and public involvement. Project report*, Bristol: University of the West of England.

NIHR (National Institute for Health Research) (2012) *Patients and public*, London: NIHR. Available at: http://www.crncc.nihr.ac.uk/ppi (accessed 22 April 2012).

Nolan, M., Hanson, E., Grant, G. and Keady, J. (2007) 'Introduction: what counts as knowledge, whose knowledge counts? Towards authentic participatory enquiry', in M. Nolan, E. Hanson, G. Grant and J. Keady (eds) *User participation in health and social care research: voices, values and evaluation*, Maidenhead: Open University Press and McGraw-Hill, pp 1–13.

Oliver, S., Rees, R., Clarke-Jones, L., Milne, R., Oakley, A., Gabbay, J., Stein, K., Buchanan, P. and Gyte, G. (2008) 'A multidimensional conceptual framework for analysing public involvement in health services research', *Health Expectations*, vol 11, no 1, pp 72–84.

Rose, D. (2004) 'Telling different stories: user involvement in mental health research', *Research and Policy Planning*, vol 22, no 2, pp 23–30.

Shields, G., Wainwright, R. and Grant, G. (2007) 'Doing user research: narratives of mental health service user researchers', in M. Nolan, E. Hanson, G. Grant and J. Keady (eds) *User participation in health and social care research: voices, values and evaluation*, Maidenhead: Open University Press and McGraw-Hill, pp 120–33.

Staley, K. (2009) *Exploring impact: public involvement in NHS, public health and social care research*, Eastleigh: INVOLVE.

Staniszewska, S., Jones, N., Marshall, S. and Newburn, M. (2007) 'User involvement in the development of a research bid: barriers, enablers and impacts', *Health Expectations*, vol 10, no 2, pp 173–83.

Thompson, J., Barber, R., Ward, P., Boote, J., Cooper, C., Armitage, C. and Jones, G. (2009) 'Health researchers' attitudes towards public involvement in health research', *Health Expectations*, vol 12, no 2, pp 209–20.

UK Mental Health Research Network (2011) 'Mental health researchers' toolkit for involving service users in the research process'. Available at: http://www.mhrn.info/pages/guidance-and-policy-publications.html (accessed 22 April 2012).

UWE (University of the West of England) (2010) *Public involvement in research: guidelines for good practice*, Bristol: UWE. Available at: http://hls.uwe.ac.uk/suci/Data/Sites/1/heifposter.pdf (accessed 22 April 2012).

Ward, P., Thompson, J., Barber, R., Armitage, C., Boote, J., Cooper, C. and Jones, G. (2010) 'Critical perspectives on "consumer" involvement in health research: epistemological dissonance and the know–do gap', *Journal of Sociology*, vol 46, no 1, pp 63–82.

FIVE

# How does who we are shape the knowledge we produce? Doing collaborative research about personality disorders

*Steve Gillard, Kati Turner and Marion Neffgen*

## Introduction

A strong tradition of involving people with lived experiences of using mental health services as active members of research teams has emerged over the last two decades. This has focused on adding the voice of personal experience to the research process and on introducing the idea of 'service user- or survivor-produced knowledge' (Sweeney et al, 2009). However, the epistemological value of these new means of knowledge production continues to be evaluated alongside the 'gold standard' of university-produced clinical-academic research about mental health (Staley, 2009). Parallel developments in the philosophy of science have introduced the concept of 'co-produced' knowledge, where the inclusion of research partners from outside of the university questions the university's monopoly as the arbiter of 'good science' (Gibbons et al, 1994). All knowledge is held to be socially accountable, and all research voices – not just the new lay arrivals – are placed on the same critical plane (Nowotny et al, 2001).

Understanding the contribution of service user researchers to mental health research becomes not just a question of 'What difference do *they* make?' but an interrogation of how who we *all* are, as academics, clinicians and service users, shapes the knowledge we produce. Efforts have been made to measure the extent to which researchers with different backgrounds – service user researchers and 'conventional' university researchers – do mental health research differently, both in the collection and analysis of interview data (Gillard et al, 2010; Rose et al, 2011). In other research, we have attempted to capture the different sense we make of our data – the different analytical narratives we produce as service user, clinical and university researchers – and how we have endeavoured to co-produce a joint narrative through a collaborative research process (Gillard et al, 2011). In this chapter, we aim to illustrate and interrogate further this collaborative research process, focusing on the analysis of qualitative interview data, in order to explore at the level of research team practice how who we are shapes the knowledge we produce.

## The research project

In this chapter, we will consider a research project entitled 'Understanding personality disorders and recovery', commissioned by a peer-led organisation that provides personality disorders services and is an active partner in the development of personality disorders policy in the UK. In the UK, principles of mental health recovery (Anthony, 1993) are increasingly informing mental health policy and service provision (Department of Health, 2011). The language of recovery is largely absent from the research literature on personality disorders, although a strong parallel tradition has existed since the 1950s – for example, in the Therapeutic Community movement (eg Dickey and Ware, 2008) – which has insisted that personality disorders are treatable and that good outcomes for individuals are possible. This project set out to explore understandings of the concept of recovery in the context of the lived experience of personality disorders.

## The team

Our team comprised three researchers – the authors – with contrasting clinical, university and service user backgrounds. The service user researcher – Kati – had several years of both service development and research experience and was actively involved in a peer-led organisation advocating and developing service user leadership in personality disorder services and training for health care professionals. The university researcher – Steve – was, as budget-holder for the project, 'principal investigator'. He was not an academic expert on personality disorders but had more than 10 years' experience in undertaking collaborative mental health research with service user researchers. The clinical researcher – Marion – was a core speciality trainee in Psychiatry and Psychotherapy with a number of years of clinical experience in two countries, and a high level of commitment of working psychotherapeutically with people diagnosed with personality disorders as her main area of clinical interest. We will refer to ourselves by name as well as role through the chapter. We feel that it is important to retain our personal identities in writing up the research process in order to better understand our different contributions to that process as socially located individuals.

## Methods

We conducted in-depth interviews with six people using a specialist personality disorders service in a London mental health NHS Trust. The specialist service provided open-access peer support groups for people living in the community who either had a diagnosis of personality disorder/s or who identified with issues associated with personality disorders. To ensure that there was variation in the people we interviewed, we selected three men and three women with an age range of 26–65, five of whom identified as white, while one female interviewee identified as Other (non-specified), roughly reflecting the demographic profile of people using the service. Interviewees attended three different peer support groups in different geographical areas, and half of them had also used other specialist personality disorders services. All of the interviewees had been attending the peer support groups for two or more years and all had received various forms of non-specialised mental health care over a long period. The service user researcher visited the peer support groups and talked to staff and service users about the research; interviews were arranged with service users who consented to participate in the study. Ethical approval for the study was given by an NHS Research Ethics Committee.

We used an interview schedule developed in an earlier project that explored understandings of recovery in a range of specialist mental health services settings (Turton et al, 2011). Marion and Kati, as clinical and service user researchers, jointly conducted all interviews, alternating in the lead interviewer role to ensure that the data was not shaped predominantly by the priorities of either researcher. We describe the process of analysing interview data in detail later. All members of the team kept reflective diaries of the whole research process. We use our diaries, together with a documentary record of the analysis process to explore our collaborative approach to research. We will not report substantive findings of the research here; these are detailed in our report to the research funders (Turner et al, 2011).

## The analysis process

Our analysis was guided by our intention to ensure that the interpretations of all members of the research team were represented in the analysis. We devised a thematic analysis process in a series of stages, with members of the team sharing the tasks, as illustrated in Figure 5.1.

**Figure 5.1: The analysis process**

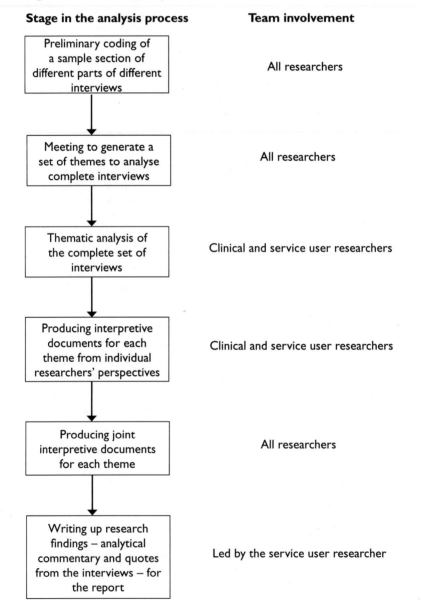

| Stage in the analysis process | Team involvement |
|---|---|
| Preliminary coding of a sample section of different parts of different interviews | All researchers |
| Meeting to generate a set of themes to analyse complete interviews | All researchers |
| Thematic analysis of the complete set of interviews | Clinical and service user researchers |
| Producing interpretive documents for each theme from individual researchers' perspectives | Clinical and service user researchers |
| Producing joint interpretive documents for each theme | All researchers |
| Writing up research findings – analytical commentary and quotes from the interviews – for the report | Led by the service user researcher |

In the preliminary stage of the analysis, all three members of the team conducted an open coding of a subsample of interview data using coding techniques common to inductive enquiry (Ritchie and Lewis, 2003). We then met to organise those codes into a set of themes, each member of the team bringing provisional suggestions for themes based on the codes we had generated in our separate preliminary analyses. Several of those themes we shared – we could agree that the descriptions and content of our themes were meaningfully similar – while others were distinctive. We brought our analyses together and, through discussion, grouped similar themes into a table that contained our different sets of codes. At a subsequent meeting, we discussed our provisional themes and agreed a final set of 15 themes (divided into three broad domains: experiencing personality disorders; personality disorders and recovery; treatment and support) that we would use to analyse the whole data set. In Table 5.1, we illustrate the development of just two of those final themes, indicating their origins in the open coding and provisional themes brought by different members of the team.

Marion and Kati then organised the entire data set by assigning data to the final set of themes. Marion and Kati undertook this part of the process because they had the best knowledge of the data and had the closest insight into personality disorders, as clinician and service user, respectively. They completed three interviews each before checking each other's analysis. We did not seek agreement through the checking process; researchers assigned additional sections of transcript to themes where they felt that the other researcher had missed something important. We took this inclusive approach to ensure that the insight of neither researcher was lost at this stage of the process.

This produced a set of theme documents populated with data from the transcripts. Marion and Kati then separately wrote interpretations of the theme documents comprising a number of statements – typically around five per theme – which they felt captured interviewees' experiences and perspectives as represented in the data. Each statement was supported with examples from the data. Statements comprising our separate interpretations are illustrated in Table 5.2 using our internal theme as an example.

**Table 5.1: Development of themes through team discussion**

| Final theme | Provisional themes | Service user researcher's codes | Clinical researcher's codes | University researcher's codes |
|---|---|---|---|---|
| *The internal experience of personality disorders (INTERNAL)* This theme comprises things we had coded under 'personal experience of personality disorders' as well as those personal responses to the external world we had coded under 'relationship with external world/social difficulties' (ie the linking we discussed; how the individual responds internally to external experience) as well as relevant aspects we had coded under 'history'. | Personal experience of personality disorders (service user researcher's theme) | Introspection Anxiety Inadequacy Avoidance Depression (intense) Self-hate Rapid mood changes, irregularity Psychotic episodes Intensity and severity of feelings Paranoia, fear Isolation, detachment | | |
| *Relating to the external world (EXTERNAL)* This theme comprises accounts of relating to concrete things in the outside world – for example: workplace; mixing with people; and dealing with bureaucracy – we had coded under 'relationship with external world/social difficulties'. It also includes relevant aspects we had coded under 'history'. | Relationship with external world (service user researcher's theme) + Social difficulties (clinical researcher's theme) | Social phobias Workplace Mixing with people Negative effect of outside world Paralysis Alienation, not part of things Dealing with the public Fear of outside world Hiding real self Impact of outside world Unsafe place, damaging, harmful System | Emotional affects – anxiety, fear, anger, relief Space vs contact Effect of other people on emotional state Effect of dealings with bureaucracy Safety, home and protection vs outside threats | Talking to someone Activity |
| History (shared theme) | History (shared theme) | Long term patterns Getting better, getting worse Childhood factors contributing to personality disorders | History | Life history |

**Table 5.2: Service user researcher's and clinical researcher's interpretations of the 'internal' theme**

| Internal theme | |
| --- | --- |
| *Service user researcher's interpretation* | *Clinical researcher's interpretation* |
| 1. Feeling alienated and isolated, dislocated from the world and from oneself. Isolation as a 'double-edged sword'; a conscious choice to withdraw as a refuge from the world in order to keep oneself safe. (NB This theme overlaps with *External*.)<br>2. Experiencing intense and polarised emotions – a roller-coaster ride of unpredictability and chaos.<br>3. The severity of personality disorders; behaving in extreme ways that carry a high risk of threat to life.<br>4. A very uncertain and vulnerable sense of self characterised by varying levels of panic, anxiety, confusion, indecision, paralysis, fear, over-reliance and dependence.<br>5. A very negative and punitive relationship with oneself, characterised by feelings of self-hatred, low self-esteem and self-criticism. | 1. **Feeling state:** The basic feeling state seems to be characterised by low mood with underlying negativity, and a state of heightened anxiety, especially in relation to social encounters and activities in public (eg public transport, going shopping, etc); additionally, people with personality disorders experience rapid changes in mood, ranging from extreme states of anxiety, depression, suicidal thoughts and behaviour, to psychotic and manic-like states; these seem to come quickly, often without obvious triggers or predictability.<br>2. **Sense of self:** The sense of self is deeply affected and uncertain; this leads to feelings of not knowing oneself, not knowing what is normal, not knowing what is wrong with oneself; and not believing in oneself or trusting one's own judgement. It is also connected with feelings of inadequacy, self-criticism and self-hatred.<br>3. **Becoming a recluse:** People describe periods (of weeks or months) where they isolate themselves and everyday things become a terrible struggle to the extent that they self-neglect, do not get out of bed, eat, drink or wash, and cannot sleep; these seem to be a reaction to their internal state and/or a result of things that happened in the external world.<br>4. **Brain:** People with personality disorders seem to feel that something is not right with their brain, that it is not functioning 'normally'; this refers to feelings of confusion, dysfunction, disorder and the feeling that the mind does not switch off.<br>5. **Self-inflicted difficulties vs difficulties with self-protection:** People with personality disorders seem to experience uncertainty and anxiety about whether difficulties are self-inflicted or deserved, as well as a realisation that there is an element of self-destruction. Added to this is a feeling that self-protective mechanisms are maybe not functioning so well. (I find it difficult to phrase this point.)<br>6. There is also something about **black and white thinking** or behaviour – becoming fixated and obsessed with something or totally despondent and disinterested. (I couldn't quite make it out and haven't elaborated on this point.) |

Our first attempt at joint interpretation involved Steve, the university researcher, producing a set of 'combined' statements for each theme, but we were not satisfied that this approach was productive of joint interpretation (see Reflections later). In our next attempt, we discussed the separate interpretations of each theme in detail as a team, sketched out what each joint interpretation would look like and shared the themes between us to write up before bringing the joint interpretations back to the team for final validation. The full set of jointly interpreted theme documents produced as a result was then used as a resource for writing the final project report (Turner et al, 2011). The joint interpretation of our internal theme is illustrated in Table 5.3 as an example.

**Table 5.3: Our joint interpretation of the 'internal' theme**

| Joint interpretation: internal theme |
|---|
| 1. People with a diagnosis of personality disorders very often (if not always) experience feelings of extreme isolation and alienation – both in relation and as a reaction to the outside world and to one's self (in terms of feeling dislocated and disassociated). This sense of isolation and alienation is often experienced as a conflict: there is a conscious choice to withdraw into oneself and rely on one's own resources in order to keep oneself safe from a world often perceived as harmful and threatening; however, at the same time, there is a recognition that conscious withdrawal from the world can be harmful and hamper well-being and recovery (examples being self-neglect and lack of basic self-care, such as eating, sleeping, washing, etc). |
| 2. People with a diagnosis of personality disorders experience intense and polarised emotions: a roller-coaster ride of unpredictability and chaos. People experience rapid changes in mood, which can range from extreme states of anxiety, depression, hyper-sensitivity, suicidal thoughts and behaviour, to psychotic, euphoric and manic-like states. These emotions seem to arrive quickly, often without obvious triggers or predictability. People often think in a very polarised, 'black and white' way. |
| 3. People with a diagnosis of personality disorders can (due to the feelings described above) behave in extreme ways that often carry a high risk of threat to life. These can be self-inflicted and destructive, such as: abusing alcohol and drugs; self-harm; and overdosing on prescribed/unprescribed medication. These behaviours are often seen as an escape or a solution from intolerable feelings, the 'lesser of two evils'. |
| 4. People with a diagnosis of personality disorders have a very uncertain and vulnerable sense of self, often characterised by varying levels of panic, anxiety, confusion, indecision, paralysis, fear, over-reliance and dependence. People feel unsure of who they are, of not knowing what is 'normal'; of not knowing what is wrong with oneself; not believing in oneself or trusting one's own judgement. Sometimes, people with this diagnosis feel that something is not right with their brain and that they are not functioning 'normally'; that they cannot control their mind or switch it off. |
| 5. People with a diagnosis of personality disorders experience a very negative and punitive relationship with themselves. This is characterised by feelings of self-hatred, low self-esteem and self-criticism. |

## Reflections

While the focus of this chapter is on our analysis process, we felt that it was important to reflect briefly on how our joint approach to interviewing, with Marion and Kati interviewing together (as clinical and service user researcher, respectively), shaped the data we produced for analysis. Marion and Kati felt not only that they had worked well together, but also that the follow-up questions they asked during interviews reflected their different backgrounds and were complementary. Kati, in particular, noted in her reflective diary how her personal experiences informed her interviewing: 'There was quite a lot that I could identify with in the interview and I tried to strike a balance between empathising and using my experience to ask other questions without leading the interviewee too much'.

We asked interviewees what they thought about the interview process and whether they thought what they told us was shaped by either the clinical or service user researcher. Interviewees found that the presence of a service user researcher enabled them to talk about their experiences:

> "an ex-service user, it just sort of brings down all my barriers so I think it's allowed me to talk more freely and feel much more comfortable." (Interviewee 4)

> "I haven't thought, 'Oh, I don't want to speak to you about things', quite the opposite." (Interviewee 5)

There was some ambivalence expressed about the impact of having a doctor as part of the interviewing team, while other interviewees were reassured by this, or did not feel that this had an effect on what they chose to talk about:

> "It puts my barriers up a little bit. I suppose it's reassuring that you obviously have an interest and experience in the field, so it's better than seeing just a general doctor but it's still slight anxiety … not that I'd be disingenuous or intentionally dishonest but … I would censor what I'd said a little bit more I think." (Interviewee 4)

> "I thought when I heard that you were coming, you are a doctor, it's good to have someone with medical experience." (Interviewee 6)

> "No, I don't think so, I honestly think I've been as honest as I can today. I'm not aware of holding things back." (Interviewee 1)

On balance, it seemed that interviewees valued being interviewed by researchers who were committed to listening to and understanding their experiences of personality disorders (whether as clinical or service user researcher) and that together the researchers had made them feel comfortable enough to talk openly about sometimes difficult experiences. We felt that a broad, comprehensive range of data was collected as a result of the joint interviewing approach, reflecting both interviewees' feelings and experiences of personality disorders and recovery.

In reflecting on the analysis process, we had recourse to our reflective diaries that we kept over the course of the project. As illustrated in the documentary record earlier, we noted tensions at various stages of the process, both when initially developing our themes and when we were producing joint interpretations:

> Some of our themes coincided but there were also marked differences, in particular relating to my 'insider' perspective where I identified themes which the other researchers understandably found difficult to relate to. (Kati)

> I felt it was difficult to let go of some things where I thought my way of interpreting was different or it made more sense, at least to me. I think that Kati felt similar about some of her points and I was aware that maybe we were each holding on to details which in the end were not really differences. (Marion)

Steve, as the university researcher, took on the role of managing the process and initially attempted to find resolutions to apparent tensions between the interpretive perspectives of the clinical and service user researchers:

> When we were making decisions about themes and coding I assumed, wrongly, that Kati and Marion had reached some kind of sticking point in their different interpretations of the data and I began to try and impose what I thought was a practical alternative approach. I stopped myself and took a step back from the analysis to let them get on with it and I think what emerged was a lot more meaningful as a result. (Steve)

Kati, as the service user researcher, reflected more than once in her diary entries on the importance of the preliminary stage of the analysis when we moved, through discussion, from our provisional themes to the final set of themes that would shape the subsequent analysis. Our 'internal' and 'external' themes were strongly advocated for by Kati at this stage of the process:

> I had some strong feelings about how I thought (and wanted) the data to be grouped and what it was telling me. I knew I had these feelings because I related very personally to the data I was dealing with.... Some people described things in a way that felt almost identical to how I might have described them if someone had asked me the same questions ... I don't attribute my response purely to having had similar experiences, but I do think my proximity to the experiences and subject matter meant that an extra 'level' or layer of sensibility and vulnerability was uncovered within me. (Kati)

> I remember being very vocal in the group meetings and quite insistent at times. It wasn't that I disagreed with what Steve and Marion were saying, more that I felt I had a perspective which they could not share and that it was incredibly important that this perspective did not get submerged or absorbed so much into our joint perspective that it lost its uniqueness. (Kati)

We reflected on our first, unsuccessful attempt to combine the individual interpretive documents:

> It became clear that our initial idea that Steve would simply be able to take both our interpretations and combine them did not work. It felt like it lost some of the essence. So we came to the conclusion that we either had to discuss it between the three of us and then either of us could try and write an account of that, or it had to be either Kati or myself as we were much more closely into the themes. (Marion)

> It took time to work out what we were doing and what worked best: some of the things we tried felt quite complicated and laborious: at the time of writing we are working in a way which seems to be working (after a

certain amount of trial and error!). We have reached this position through a lot of group discussion and pooling of our individual experiences in working with the data. (Kati)

Steve acknowledged that his direct contribution to the analysis reduced as he increasingly took on a more technical role of providing methodological support to the project, especially when the analysis became protracted and difficult:

> I became less directly involved in the project, and that has felt like a good thing as the service user researcher and clinical researcher have come to work so well together ... because they are both very committed to understanding personality disorders they seem to 'get' each other in ways that are a bit lost on me sometimes. I find myself facilitating their research conversation by guiding the process onto the next stage, but that feels entirely appropriate. (Steve)

## Discussion: how who we are shaped the knowledge we produced in our research

At the beginning of this chapter, we set out to interrogate how who we are as researchers shaped the knowledge we produced in a research project about personality disorders and recovery. We have illustrated this with a documentary record of key stages of the analysis process and our personal reflections on that process. We wanted to explore how the knowledge generated through this research project was socially accountable (Nowotny et al, 2001) in terms of our different locations as university, clinical and service user researchers. We described the university researcher, Steve, as technical lead for the project, stepping back from imposing methodological solutions to the challenges we encountered in the analysis process and taking on a more facilitative role enabling the team as a whole to explore potential interpretations of the data together. The service user researcher, Kati, argued strongly that a lived experience perspective should guide and shape our analysis from an early stage. Kati made explicit use of personal resonance with interviewees' experiences, as recounted in the data, to inform her articulation of a bifurcation of lived experience as a hostile external world and the troubled refuge of the internal world. The clinical researcher, Marion, spoke of 'letting go' of some of the sense she had made of the data, and we might speculate that a clinician in a later stage of their career would experience greater difficulty in doing so. Nonetheless, Marion's interpretation remains intact in our analysis in the foregrounding of the damaged sense of self and of distressed feeling states (see Tables 5.2 and 5.3), and is more explicitly present in a number of our other themes around the importance of supporting the development of positive relationships through therapeutic work in personality disorders services.

In other work (Gillard et al, 2012), we have wondered if it is our collective and deliberate reflection on our social locations as researchers that has enabled us to co-produce knowledge through collaborative research. Other researchers (Mauther and Doucet, 2008) have cautioned that the collaborative nature of research can be undermined where 'field/contextual'-based knowledge is separated from 'office/textual' knowledge through the division of labour within the team, and where relational aspects of teamwork are neglected. We did separate some of our tasks – reflecting both the closeness to the data of clinical and service user researchers, and the more methodological role of the university researcher – but not at the expense of dialogue within the team. Patterson et al (2010) describe a 'dialogic collaborative process' that stresses the importance not just of active self-awareness at both individual and team level, but also of the commitment of each research team member to dialogue if the impact of epistemological tensions on the research process are to be understood. The literary concept of *heteroglossia* – that within a spoken language, different strata of meaning coexist as (socially located) discourses or narratives – has been applied to understanding the way in which multidisciplinary health care teams function (Goldsmith et al, 2010). That sense of heterogeneity of meaning was palpable in our research team, both when we first brought our preliminary analyses to the team, and also when the university researcher initially attempted to combine the clinical and service user researchers' separate interpretations. At both points in the process, it was only through strenuous dialogue within the team, and through explicit acknowledgement of 'where we were coming from' in offering our interpretations, that we managed to move beyond those epistemological tensions and co-produce our analysis.

## How this approach informs collaborative research about personality disorders

Research in the field of medical anthropology has suggested that, through discourse about our physical health – in the context of medical treatment – we 'resist' the medicalisation of our bodies and co-produce our own local biologies (Lock, 2001).That there is, as such, a moral discourse of treatment has also been explored in the field of psychiatry (Brodwin, 2008), while, elsewhere, use of a third person to mediate the doctor–patient discourse in the diagnostic interview has been employed to explore the potential for a diagnostic practice that is sensitive to the patient's 'inner experience' of pain and suffering (Katz and Shotter, 1996).

This notion of diagnosis as a product of an institutionalised discourse, and of the discourse of lived experience as a source of 'resistance' to the pathologising of emotional distress, has been explored in depth in the context of the current medical diagnosis of Borderline Personality Disorder (Wirth-Cauchon, 2000). Recent attempts in the UK to move on from a historical set of assumptions about the untreatability of personality disorders (Lewis and Appleby, 1988) and to understand better the experience of personality disorders – for example, the Department of Health and Ministry of Justice sponsored National Knowledge and Understanding Framework (see www. personalitydisorder.org.uk) – articulate this moral discourse at the level of policy and practice.What this chapter has illustrated is the potential to 'trouble' (Lock, 2001) the diagnostic category that is personality disorder; to co-produce, through both our self-conscious reflection on who we are and our commitment to discursive research practice as a team, a new narrative that captures the lived experience of personality disorders *in the context of* treatment practice and recovery policy in the UK.This enterprise has been referred to in the literature cited earlier as 'moral discourse'. Kati, the service user researcher on our team, insisted that the discourse of lived experience should not be submerged; indeed, that it should shape our joint endeavour. Steve, the university researcher, as the third person in our process, acted to ensure that what we produced remained sensitive to both Marion's clinical perspective and Kati's lived experience perspective.

Clinical guidance in the UK, nearly 10 years old now (National Institute of Mental Health England, 2003), has stipulated that staff working in personality disorders need to develop skills – such as reflective practice and treatment alliance – to support people experiencing personality disorders. Our collaborative approach to 'knowing personality disorders' models some of those skills rather than presenting a revised phenomenology for the clinician to apply through their practice. We conclude that it is not just 'who we are' that shapes the knowledge that we produce. The moral, discursive practice we enacted within the collaborative team was productive of new understandings of the lived experience of personality disorders and is of applied relevance to medical practitioners.

## References

Anthony, W. (1993) 'Recovery from mental illness: the guiding vision of the mental health service system in the 1990s', *Psychosocial Rehabilitation Journal*, vol 16, pp 11–23.

Brodwin, P. (2008) 'The coproduction of moral discourse in U.S. community psychiatry', *Medical Anthropology Quarterly*, vol 22, no 2, pp 127–47.

Department of Health (2011) *No health without mental health: a cross-government mental health outcomes strategy for people of all ages*, London: Department of Health.

Dickey, B. and Ware, N. (2008) 'Therapeutic communities and mental health system reform', *Psychiatric Rehabilitation Journal*, vol 32, pp 105–9.

Gibbons, M., Limoges, C., Nowotny, H., Schwatrzman, S., Scott, P. and Trow, M. (eds) (1994) *The new production of knowledge*, London: Sage.

Gillard, S., Borschmann, R., Turner, K., Goodrich-Purnell, N., Lovell, K. and Chambers, M. (2010) 'What difference does it make? Finding evidence of the impact of mental health service user researchers on research into the experiences of detained psychiatric patients', *Health expectations*, vol 13, no 2, pp 185–94.

Gillard, S., Borschmann, R., Turner, K., Goodrich-Purnell, N., Lovell, K. and Chambers, M. (2011) 'Producing different analytical narratives, coproducing integrated analytical narrative: a qualitative study of UK detained mental health patient experiences involving service user researchers', *International Journal of Social Research Methodology*, vol 15, no 3, pp 239–54, DOI: 10.1080/13645579.2011.572673.

Gillard, S., Simons, L., Turner, K., Lucock, M. and Edwards, C. (2012) 'Patient and public involvement in the coproduction of knowledge: reflection on the analysis of qualitative data in a mental health study', *Qualitative Health Research*, vol 22, no 8, pp 1126–37, DOI: 10.1177/1049732312448541.

Goldsmith, J., Wittenberg-Lyles, E., Rodriguez, D. and Sanchez-Reilly, S. (2010) 'Interdisciplinary geriatric and palliative care team narratives: collaboration practices and barriers', *Qualitative Health Research*, vol 20, pp 93–104.

Katz, A. and Shotter, J. (1996) 'Hearing the patient's "voice": toward a social poetics in diagnostic interviews', *Social Science & Medicine*, vol 43, no 6, pp 919–31.

Lewis, G. and Appleby, L. (1988) 'Personality disorder: the patients psychiatrists dislike', *British Journal of Psychiatry*, vol 153, pp 44–9.

Lock, M. (2001) 'The tempering of medical anthropology: troubling natural categories', *Medical Anthropology Quarterly*, vol 15, no 4, pp 478–92.

Mauthner, N. and Doucet, A. (2008) '"Knowledge once divided can be hard to put together again": an epistemological critique of collaborative and team-based research practices', *Sociology*, vol 42, pp 971–85.

National Institute of Mental Health England (2003) *Breaking the cycle of rejection: the personality disorder capabilities framework*, London: Department of Health.

Nowotny, H., Scott, P. and Gibbons, M. (eds) (2001) *Rethinking science*, Cambridge: Polity Press.

Patterson, S., Hart, J. and Weaver, T. (2010) 'Delusions and qualitative confusions: a dialogic collaborative exploration', *Qualitative Health Research*, vol 20, pp 1008–18.

Ritchie, J. and Lewis, J. (eds) (2003) *Qualitative research practice: a guide for social science students and researchers*, London: Sage.

Rose, D., Leese, M., Oliver, D., Sidhu, R., Bennewith, O., Priebe, S. and Wykes, T. (2011) 'A comparison of participant information elicited by service user and non-service user researchers', *Psychiatric Services*, vol 62, no 2, pp 210–13, DOI: 10.1176/appi.ps.62.2.210.

Staley, K. (2009) *Exploring impact: public involvement in NHS, public health and social care research*, Eastleigh: INVOLVE.

Sweeney, A., Beresford, P., Faulkner, A., Nettle, M. and Rose, D. (2009) *This is survivor research*, Ross-On-Wye: PCCS Books.

Turner, K., Neffgen, M. and Gillard, S. (2011) *Understanding personality disorders and recovery*, London: Emergence.

Turton, P., Demetriou, A., Boland, W., Gillard, S., Kavuma, M., Mezey, G., Mountford, V., Turner, K., White, S., Zadeh, E. and Wright, C. (2011) 'One size fits all: or horses for courses? Recovery-based care in specialist mental health services', *Social Psychiatry and Psychiatric Epidemiology*, vol 46, no 2, pp 127–36.

Wirth-Cauchon, J. (2000) 'A dangerous symbolic mobility: narratives of borderline personality disorder', in D. Fee (ed) *Pathology and the postmodern: mental illness as discourse and experience*, London: Sage.

# SIX

# Where do service users' knowledges sit in relation to professional and academic understandings of knowledge?

*Peter Beresford and Kathy Boxall*

## Introduction

The focus of this chapter is the 'experiential knowledge' of mental health service users and the part it has played and can play in shaping mental health thinking, policy, practice, research, education and services. Our aim is to explore service users' experiential knowledge – or perhaps we should say knowledges, since there is no one homogeneous service user knowledge – in more depth, and to situate this discussion within broader sociological understandings of knowledge production. The chapter draws on feminist and disability movement critiques of traditional social research to examine academic and professional understandings of knowledge and their role in relation to service user knowledges. Finally, we conclude by considering the impact of service user knowledges on ways in which madness and distress can be understood.

Before we begin this discussion, we first need to say something about ourselves; the two of us have direct personal experience as users or recipients of mental health services and currently work as social work educators in British universities. Our contact with the psychiatric system has been hallmarked by 'personal tragedy' understandings of madness and distress, underpinned firmly by a perceived biomedical 'impairment of the mind' (Oliver, 1990). The challenging of unhelpful individual deficit approaches to understanding madness and distress provides a starting point for this chapter, so too does our desire to challenge the conventional epistemological separations of 'us' and 'them' – those who make knowledge about mental health service users and those about whom such knowledge is made. However, we are also clear that although we speak from our own experience, we cannot speak for other mental health service users, and writing a chapter that situates service users' knowledges in relation to wider understandings of knowledge inevitably leads to ambiguities and confusions when, as authors, we occupy dual positions as 'knowers' and 'known'. This has led to difficult decisions about 'voice'. In the interests of clarity – although at the risk of reinforcing the putative objectivity of 'academic voice' – we have written about service users as 'them'. Anomalies of this nature are, of course, the very issues with which this chapter is concerned in its exploration of the place of service user knowledges in relation to conventional academic and professional understandings of what constitutes knowledge.

## Experiential knowledge

The key quality that distinguishes mental health service user knowledges from all others involved in the field of madness and mental health is that they are *experiential*. As Borkman (1976, p 446) has put it: 'Experiential knowledge is truth learned from personal experience with a phenomenon rather than truth acquired by discursive reasoning, observation or reflection on information provided by others'. Thus, service users 'know' from their direct experience. Their knowledge has been described in different ways: as experiential or direct knowledge; as lived experience; and as from 'experts by experience'. Cotterell and Morris (2012, p 58) highlight two important elements of experiential knowledge: first, that 'it arises from personal participation in the phenomenon and incorporates a reflective stance on this experience'; and, second, that the individual holds belief and trust in this knowledge based on their experience of the phenomenon in question.

Service users' knowledge alone is defined by and primarily based on direct *experience* of madness and distress and associated policy and provision *from the receiving end*. It grows out of their personal and collective experience of policy, practice and services. This is not to deny the existence or validity of 'practitioner' or 'carer' knowledge(s) or the fact that they are based on direct experience. However, they are based on direct experience of being a practitioner or carer, not of experiencing madness and distress or the psychiatric system, as are service user knowledges. Service user knowledges are not based solely on an intellectual, analytical, occupational or political concern.

Traditionally, however, mental health policy, practice and research have been dominated by such 'expert' knowledge, whether framed as scientific, professional, academic, research or psychiatric knowledge.

Academics from a range of disciplines (eg psychiatry, psychology, education, sociology, social policy, history), as well as numerous different professional groups (eg psychiatrists, psychologists, psychiatric nurses, social workers, criminologists, lawyers), have laid claim to specialist knowledge resulting from academic research or 'practice' in the area of 'mental health'.

Mental health service users have historically been excluded from the knowledge-production processes of psychiatry and the mental health system. Knowledge about mental health service users has been produced by people without mental health problems or at least who do not identify as such, or have a history of using mental health services. Such 'knowledge' has been underpinned by and has highlighted individual 'deficit', 'deviance' and 'pathology', and has been used for many years to justify the segregation and institutionalisation of mental health service users. The dominant epistemology has worked to prohibit mental health service users from being producers or knowers of their own knowledges. Psychiatric knowledge has been based on the 'knowledge claims' of others about the experience of mad people and mental health service users. They have played the key role in interpreting service users' experience, while the latter's own interpretations have, as has been argued, been excluded or devalued.

## The broader context of disability

It should be said that this situation is not unique to mental health service users. It is also the case for a wide range of disabled people, including people with learning difficulties, people with physical and sensory impairments, and older people. The same process has applied of ignoring or excluding their experiential knowledge, producing knowledge framed in terms of 'deficit' and 'specialness' and medicalising and pathologising such groups (Oliver, 1990, 1996; Thomas and Loxley, 2001; Oliver and Barnes, 2012). Thus, while the issues explored in this chapter in relation to service users' knowledge focus particularly on mental health and mental health service users, in many cases, they apply more broadly across disability issues and disabled groups. This is not to say, of course, that there are not differences between these groups and that each does not have its own unique history, identity, concerns and, indeed, knowledges.

Medicalised individual models of disability have predominated across different disability categories and groups, including mental health service users. This has been particularly developed in psychiatry, which has created an ever-extending range of diagnostic categories, often tautological, framing social phenomena in medical terms, ranging from 'conduct disorder' to 'attention deficit hyperactivity disorder' (ADHD), 'narcissistic personality disorder' and 'internet addiction' (Brown, 1990). Disabled activists and academics have highlighted the problems of an individual/medical model approach to understanding disability and have instead emphasised social approaches, proposing a social model of disability (Oliver, 1990, 1996). This highlights the disabling social barriers imposed on people with impairments as well as the complex relationships between such disability and impairment (Thomas, 2007).

This has led to the development by disabled people of an emancipatory research paradigm (Oliver, 1992; Mercer, 2002; Barnes, 2003), which, underpinned by social model epistemology, focuses research on disabling barriers rather than individual deficits. This has found similar expression among mental health service users/ survivors, who have developed user-controlled and 'survivor research'. While mental health service users have not developed their own equivalent of the social model of disability, they have nonetheless both highlighted their concerns about the damaging effects of prevailing medicalised understandings and also argued for and supported more social approaches to both interpreting and responding to mental health problems (Beresford et al, 2010).

## The broader context of user involvement

It is the development of service user research that has brought the issue of user or experiential knowledge to prominence and highlighted the role and significance of experiential knowledge. But this, in turn, needs to be considered in the broader context of 'user' or 'public and patient' involvement in politics, public policy and practice. There has been increasing interest in and emphasis on such involvement internationally in policy and politics. This has been developed in many areas, including professional education and practice, policymaking, management, service planning, research, and evaluation.

Different competing ideologies, models and understandings of user involvement have developed within the framework of this terminology. While these have taken many forms, at least one key distinction can be drawn. This is between:

- the consumerist/market-inspired involvement that has grown in significance since the shift to the political right in countries like the UK that took place from the 1980s; and

- the emergence of service user movements, starting with the disabled people's movement in the 1970s, with their interest in involvement to increase their say and control and democratise policy and services (Beresford, 2002).

There have been different, if overlapping, strands of interest in such user involvement, with the former advanced by the state and service system and the latter by service users, their organisations and their supporters (Campbell and Oliver, 1996; Beresford and Campbell, 2004; Campbell, 2009; Beresford, 2012).

This has also been reflected in the emergence of interest in user involvement in knowledge development and exchange. This has mainly focused on user involvement in research, although knowledge development extends beyond this, of course, having both individual and collective expressions. What distinguishes discussion about user involvement in the context of research and knowledge production is that it is ultimately concerned with knowledge that is based on direct or 'lived' experience. It is, as we have seen, concerned with experiential knowledge or *knowledges*.

Service user knowledges have become both more visible and more influential. Yet, at the same time, they remain contested and contentious and continue to be marginalised. They face ideological, professional and methodological barriers that have without doubt inhibited their development, as well as encouraged their exclusion. It is these barriers that we want to explore in more detail next.

## Experiential knowledge and competing ideologies

It is important to recognise that recent increased interest in service user knowledge is part of broader pressures to increase user involvement. These pressures, however, are highly ambiguous in nature. The prevailing consumerist interest in involvement from state and service systems is still largely concerned with obtaining the views and ideas of service users as a *data source* to inform its activities and decision-making, in the same way that the market checks out customer preferences through market research. There is no suggestion that user knowledge has any greater value than this and its analysis and interpretation remains with traditional power-holders. In this way, it is no different to traditional mental health research, where service users have mainly only featured as a data source, with analysis and findings offered by non-service user researchers, reflecting their professional and research perspectives.

This is in sharp contrast to service user approaches to involvement that are concerned with democratisation and empowerment and that prioritise:

• people speaking and acting for themselves;
• a shift in the locus of decision-making;
• the redistribution of power and control; and
• personal and political empowerment.

Thus, user involvement based on consumerist ideology is not necessarily consistent with, or supportive of, the inclusion and development of experiential knowledge, while the democratic model favoured by service users and their movements is implicitly and inherently concerned with its advancement. Service users getting involved in conventional consultative and participatory processes based on consumerist ideology can find themselves sucked into reinforcing the ideas, agendas and concerns of dominant traditional medicalised individual interpretations of their experience. It is not clear why service users should see advancing professional or expert knowledge in this way as consistent with developing their own knowledges and discourses. Put simply, why would it help mental health service users to get involved in traditional medicalised psychiatric research concerned with developing new drug treatments when they have constantly argued from their own experience for the importance of broader, more social focuses in developing research-based knowledge? This helps explain the growing reluctance of service users and their organisations to respond to such invitations. On the other hand, they are more likely to see collective action within their own organisations and movements as opportunities both to advance and to operationalise their experiential knowledge.

## Experiential knowledge and research methodology

Experiential knowledge and the survivor research that builds on and develops it do not sit comfortably with traditional positivist research methodology. Such methodology has emphasised and prioritised research values of 'objectivity', 'neutrality' and 'distance'. It has highlighted the 'scientific' nature of research and the potential of such a scientific and rigorous research process to produce findings that are reliable and replicable. It has come particularly to be associated with quantitative research methods. The Department of Health, for example, has supported the idea of a 'hierarchy' of evidence, with quantitative research methods like randomised controlled trials (RCTs) and systematic reviews at the top and 'expert opinion', including the views of 'service users' and 'carers', at the bottom (Department of Health, 1999; Glasby and Beresford, 2006).

Such positivist values do not sit comfortably with survivor, user-controlled or emancipatory disability research. These are explicitly partisan and political, committed to:

- supporting the empowerment of service users;
- seeking broader social change; and
- equalising the social relations of research production (Oliver, 1996; Faulkner, 2004; Sweeney et al, 2009).

They also value and prioritise the subjective experience of service users. There is now a growing body of such user-controlled research. There are large as well as smaller projects, a significant and growing literature, a developing methodology, and mixed-methods and quantitative as well as qualitative studies.

## Generating survivor knowledge

This research can be seen as both the product and producer of survivor knowledge. Mental health service users/survivors have developed research processes that they initiate, shape and undertake, drawing on their shared experience. In turn, such research has become a key means of generating and collectivising survivor knowledge, addressing issues of concern to survivors from social perspectives and creating knowledge that has previously not been available. There are now a large and growing number of such projects. With humble origins – often unfunded projects that mental health service users/researchers undertook because they knew no one else would – they have now expanded into universities as well as being undertaken in service user-led organisations. While still mainly based on qualitative methods, because of financial constraints still operating on survivor, like other user-controlled, research, they are now also developing mixed-methods and quantitative studies, local, national and international in scope (Beresford and Wallcraft, 1997; Sweeney et al, 2009).

The groundbreaking survivor research initiative was the Strategies for Living project, based at the Mental Health Foundation (Faulkner and Nicholls, 1999; Faulkner and Layzell, 2000; Nicholls, 2001). This developed major innovative programmes of work in relation to survivor research, developing research and training, building capacity, pioneering new research methods and approaches, providing funding for local projects, and developing the overall research approach. Since then, many other projects have been documented, ranging from research exploring experiences of community-based psychotherapy and peer or mentor support, to projects like that carried out at the Centre for Recovery in the University of Hertfordshire, designed from the start by someone with a diagnosis of 'bipolar disorder' who sought funding and led on research processes involving other service users along the way, for example, in reviewing the training that was being piloted (Beresford et al, 2009). While survivor research has not been associated with particular research methods, it is associated with exploring innovative methods like film, photographs and activities, including groups who might otherwise get left out, for example, deaf mental health service users, and also with developing the methods it does use to ensure that they are more participatory and help equalise relationships between researcher and researched (Faulkner, 2010).

Also important here is the work of the Service User Research Enterprise (SURE), based at the Institute of Psychiatry, where service user researchers have developed new approaches to quantitative research that are more consistent with the process, aims and values of user-controlled research. They have carried out large-scale international systematic reviews and RCTs. SURE has questioned the assumed 'neutrality' of traditional RCTs on the basis that their outcome measures are defined by clinicians, and particularly researchers, and developed a different approach based primarily on service users' views and experience. This process has now been employed in four studies, including one on acute mental health wards and another on continuity of care (Rose et al, 2008, 2009). They have undertaken an RCT exploring differences between conventional and service user interviewers and a model for developing user-generated outcome measures (Rose et al, 2011a, 2011b; Evans et al, 2012).

## The devaluing of experience-based research

However, survivor research is still not seen as passing the positivist research test. This needs to be reconsidered. Diana Rose, a survivor researcher, has suggested a way of doing this, by thinking of user research as simply coming from a different standpoint from traditional research: 'That of those who receive services and treatments.... There is no "universal knowledge" but only particular knowledges produced through different standpoints. Different standpoints produce "different truths"' (Rose, 2009, p 41).

Feminist standpoint theorists argue that traditional social science generates a reality that excludes the experiences of women, but this can be corrected by undertaking research from a feminist standpoint. A feminist standpoint is achieved by engaging in the feminist struggle in an attempt to see the world from women's point of view (Harding, 1987, 1997; Hekman, 1997). Standpoint theory opposes positivist social science's claim to objectivity. Hekman (1997, pp 346–7) characterises such objectivity 'as the separation between knower and known, removal from the situatedness of knowledge'. Such separation is a necessary constituent of modernist (masculinist) 'truth'. Harding (1997, p 382) argues that the central concern of standpoint theorists is not 'to justify the truth of feminist claims to more accurate accounts of reality. Rather, it is relations between power and knowledge that concern these thinkers'.

In relation to the social hierarchy that polices and controls the production of knowledge about madness and mental health problems, mental health service users have been firmly located at the bottom. Harding's (1993) analysis is concerned with 'marginal lives' in general, rather than mental health service users in particular. However, following through her analysis suggests that:

> [Mental health service users'] experiences and lives have been devalued or ignored as a source of objectivity maximizing questions – the answers to which are not necessarily to be found in those experiences or lives but elsewhere in the beliefs and activities of people at the center who make policies and engage in social practices that shape marginal lives. (Harding, 1993, p 54)

A standpoint is founded on commonality (Hartsock, 1997). Can mental health service users in any sense be viewed as knowers with a common standpoint? There are, of course, many differences among and within mental health service users, for example, in the treatments and regimes they experience and on the basis of gender, sexuality, ethnicity and the diagnostic category in which they are included. However, mental health service users, like other groups of disabled people, have found themselves on the receiving end of collective solutions based on perceived or accredited 'mental illness'. Collective solutions to the problem of 'mental illness' that result in the lives of mental health service users being 'regulated by the state' continue to this day. A mental health service user/survivor standpoint could bring together mental health service users (whatever the 'aetiology' of their accredited or perceived 'mental illness') on the basis that their lives have been subjected to these or similar collective 'solutions'. Adopting standpoint theorists' criteria for assessing knowledge would indicate that knowledges developed from a mental health service user/survivor standpoint should be assessed according to their challenging of injustice, their creation of cultures of resistance and their transformative potential in the lives of mental health service users.

## Excluding service users' knowledge

As we have seen, historically, service user knowledge has been marginalised in psychiatric and mental health discourse. At best, service users' experience has been used as a data source to be interpreted by supposedly expert others. This raises the issue of what negative consequences such exclusion may have.

Two sets of negatives can be postulated. The first of these are negative effects on the knowledge base itself from leaving out a unique source of knowledge. Even from a narrow consumerist standpoint, taking no account of what mental health service users want and think ignores the basic tenets of market research and makes for inefficiency. It leaves products, which are now taken to include public services, and their providers, uninformed by customer preferences. In market terms, this increases the risk of making provision that is unwanted, inappropriate and does not work (Simmons et al, 2009).

Second are the negative effects for service users, for whom such exclusion is morally and ethically unsustainable, because it represents a denial of their human and civil rights. It means that they are prevented from influencing policy and provision that specifically impacts on their lives and may have major and damaging effects on them. In addition, it means that they are effectively prevented from speaking for and about themselves (Campbell, 2009). Speaking for yourself, or self-advocacy, has emerged as the cornerstone principle of the modern disabled people's and service users' movements (Campbell and Oliver, 1996; Beresford and Campbell, 2004). As mental health service users/survivors have themselves repeatedly highlighted, being denied this opportunity tends to result in their being presented by others in distorted, patronising and pathologising ways (May, 2004; Trivedi, 2009). This is what we can expect to happen when *any* oppressed or excluded group's understandings are ignored or rejected, whether on the basis of sexuality, gender, race, age, culture, class, belief or disability. They tend to be presented as inferior, deviant or defective. The evidence also highlights that the negative effects for mental health service users/survivors are compounded if they are different in other ways, for example, in relation to gender, sexuality or race – all of which historically have resulted in inferior treatment in the psychiatric system (eg Chambers, 2009).

However, the devaluing and denial of people's viewpoints as a result of their being oppressed, or seen as different, as has been the case with mental health service users, has an additionally rarely recognised but destructive effect. It means that if someone has such an experience, they can then expect routinely to face further discrimination and be further marginalised by being seen as having less credibility and being a less reliable source of knowledge. This further invalidates people who are already heavily disadvantaged (Beresford, 2003). It means that their interpretation of themselves and their situations will always tend to be seen as inferior to those of others without their experience; a double – experiential and epistemological – discrimination.

## Tensions between expert/professional and experiential knowledge

The history of mental health service users' experiential knowledge has, as we have noted, predominantly been one of exclusion and marginalisation. These are, however, times of significant change because of the increasing interest in recent years in user involvement, rights-based public and social policy, and the challenges to discrimination mounted by service users and other identity-based groups and their movements. Having said that, there continue to be serious tensions between expert/professional and experiential knowledge, although these are often concealed from public discussion because of the prevailing rhetoric of user involvement and inclusion. Little work seems to have been done to explore these tensions more carefully and to develop an evidence base in relation to them. However, they do seem to be underpinned by several potential sources of conflict between experiential and expert/professional knowledge. These include:

- inequalities of power, legitimacy and status;
- expert/professional insecurities;
- competing values and methodologies; and
- competing interests.

The state of experiential knowledge cannot be considered in isolation from issues of inequalities of power and legitimacy that have operated in relation to it and expert/professional knowledge. Service users and service user researchers repeatedly report the inferior value and credibility attached to their knowledge. They also have much less power to support it (Turner and Beresford, 2005). Yet, each of the key professions involved in mental health – psychiatry, nursing, social work, occupational therapy and psychology – faces its own difficulties and problems of credibility and authority. None carries with it the strength and authority invested in professions like physical medicine or the law. Each has to stake its own knowledge claims and can expect to have them challenged. Some, notably social work, occupational therapy and nursing, do not have strong academic histories and are still building their credentials.

They therefore seem to face the development of user knowledge with some trepidation and uncertainty, fearful that it may further undermine their academic or 'expert' status. They have tended to see the involvement of service users and their knowledge as a zero-sum game, rather than recognising that it may provide other opportunities and roles for knowledge development for them. That is to say, they appear often to have taken the view that if experiential knowledge is given credence and included for consideration, then it will be to the detriment of their 'expert' knowledge.

Thus, historically, their role as 'knowers' of mental health issues, madness and distress seems to have been conditional on the exclusion of the direct knowledge of service users themselves, and while the latter has begun to enter the arena, there is still undoubtedly resistance to it, as is highlighted by survivor researchers (Sweeney et al, 2009). One way in which this continues is on the basis of the supposedly inferior methodological value of survivor research because it is not based on positivist research values. At the same time, significantly, there are indications that mental health and related researchers do not necessarily feel secure in their own research status. Again, this is particularly evident in health-related and social work disciplines. While they have actually been pioneers of qualitative and participatory research methodology, the inferior status granted to these approaches in some quarters means that there has also been some movement to more traditional research methodologies because of the greater conventional academic respectability associated with them. Social work offers an interesting case study of this development.

In recent years, there has been an increasing move in social work to more traditional, quantitative and mixed-methods research. This reflects social work's search for increased research respectability and enhanced funding opportunities, not least from the Economic and Social Research Council, which funded little social work research in the past. Notable examples include Oxford University's Centre for Evidence-Based

Intervention, the Tilda Goldberg Centre at Bedfordshire University and the Families and Schools Together (FAST) programme at Middlesex University. All offer a similar rationale, emphasising rigour, science and experimentation and highlighting so-called 'evidence-based' social work, which is equated with quantitative research, based on traditional RCTs and systematic reviews. Thus:

> The Centre for Evidence-Based Intervention specialises in high-quality evaluation of interventions for social and psychosocial problems, in particular through conducting randomised trials, systematic reviews and other evaluation designs. We also carry out basic research into causes of social problems, to enhance knowledge of intervention mechanisms. (From: http://www.spi.ox.ac.uk/research/centre-for-evidence-based-intervention.html)

> FAST has gained its status as an evidence based programme both by the UN, UK and US as a result of rigorous research on the effectiveness of the programme. To date four large randomised controlled trials with 1 or 2 year follow-up have been carried out that firmly evidence that FAST helps children and their families. Programme evaluation is an integral part of FAST and this is carried out using a pre–post questionnaire design using standardised instruments with established reliability and validity. (From: http://www.mdx.ac.uk/aboutus/Schools/hssc/mh-sw/research/fast.aspx)

The Tilda Goldberg Centre does also refer to user involvement in research, thus:

> The most rigorous evaluative design involves a valid comparison group. However, the practical and ethical issues in such studies are considerable. This may be in part why so few have been carried out in social work. The Goldberg Centre is centrally concerned with using and developing such methods and these are likely to make up the bulk of the work of the Centre. (From: http://www.beds.ac.uk/goldbergcentre/research)

> The Centre is particularly concerned with evaluating social work interventions and in developing the capacity for experimental and quasi-experimental approaches to such

evaluations. However, our philosophy is that experimental approaches are only one element of rigorous evaluation and that they should ideally be combined with qualitative components and the involvement of users of services in research. (From: http://www.beds.ac.uk/goldbergcentre/about)

## The contribution of experiential knowledge

Making contact with each other, working collectively in groups and organisations, has made it possible for mental health service users to develop their own collective knowledges. They have produced their own recorded body of knowledge, increasingly available to each other and other stakeholders. This provides a dynamic and developing source of experiential knowledge, making it possible to advance their own survivor discourses, to set next to and on occasion to challenge prevailing views and understandings. What starts as people's own analysis of their experience can become sophisticated and influential forms of knowledge, impacting on and fundamentally transforming received understandings (Beresford, 2003, pp 39–40).

Thus, service user knowledges have already had some significant effects. These include, for example:

- providing an additional resource for understanding, which has generated valuable re-conceptualisations by mental health service users of some of the major manifestations of madness and distress that they experience. This has led to the 'hearing voices' movement and to creative harm minimisation approaches to self-harm and eating distress, which instead of treating them as individual pathologies, puts them in their context as responses to broader oppression, discrimination and disempowerment (Campbell, 2009);
- giving rise to new responses to distress, including peer support, self-management, holistic and complementary approaches, self-run schemes for personal support, outreach and community development, and user-controlled services and organisations. These blur traditional distinctions between 'helper' and 'helped' (Beresford, 2010); and
- developing helpful, more participatory, research methodologies, in quantitative as well as qualitative research, in RCTs and systematic reviews (Rose et al, 2005, 2008).

Perhaps most important, such experiential knowledge has behind it a constituency determined to achieve the changes to which it points. This commitment to change is also embodied in the values of the mental health service user/survivor movement and the survivor research that it has pioneered.

## References

Barnes, C. (2003) 'What a difference a decade makes: reflections on doing "emancipator" disability research', *Disability & Society*, vol 18, no 1, pp 3–17.

Beresford, P. (2002) 'Participation and social policy: transformation, liberation or regulation', in R. Sykes, C. Bochel and N. Ellison (eds) *Social policy review 14*, Bristol: Policy Press/Social Policy Association, pp 265–90.

Beresford, P. (2003) *It's our lives: a short theory of knowledge, distance and experience*, London: Citizen Press in association with Shaping Our Lives.

Beresford, P. (2010) *A straight talking guide to being a mental health service user*, Ross-on-Wye: PCCS Books.

Beresford, P. (2012) 'Psychiatric system survivors: an emerging movement', in N. Watson, A. Roulstone and C. Thomas (eds) *Routledge handbook of disability studies*, London and New York, NY: Routledge, pp 151–64.

Beresford, P. and Campbell, P. (2004) 'Participation and protest: mental health service users/survivors', in M.J. Todd and G. Taylor (eds) *Democracy and participation: popular protest and new social movements*, London: Merlin Press, pp 326–42.

Beresford, P. and Wallcraft, J. (1997) 'Psychiatric system survivors and emancipatory research: issues, overlaps and differences', in C. Barnes and G. Mercer (eds) *Doing disability research*, Leeds: The Disability Press/University of Leeds, pp 67–87.

Beresford, P., Nicholls, V. and Turner, M. (2009) 'Examples of user controlled research', draft unpublished revised final report for NIHR Involve, Shaping Our Lives, London.

Beresford, P., Nettle, M. and Perring, R. (2010) *Towards a social model of madness and distress? Exploring what service users say*, York: Joseph Rowntree Foundation.

Borkmann, T. (1976) 'Experiential knowledge: a new concept for the analysis of self-help groups', *Social Services Review*, vol 50, pp 445–56.

Brown, P. (1990) 'The name game: toward a sociology of diagnosis', *Journal of Mind and Behavior*, vol 11, nos 3/4, pp 385–406.

Campbell, J. and Oliver, M. (1996) *Disability politics: understanding our past, changing our future*, London: Routledge.

Campbell, P. (2009) 'The service user/survivor movement', in J. Reynolds, R. Muston, T. Heller, J. Leach, M. McCormick, J. Wallcraft and M. Walsh (eds) *Mental health still matters*, Basingstoke: Palgrave, pp 46–52.

Chambers, P. (2009) 'What black women want from the mental health system', in J. Reynolds, R. Muston, T. Heller, J. Leach, M. McCormick, J. Wallcraft and M. Walsh (eds) *Mental health still matters*, Basingstoke: Palgrave, pp 228–30.

Cotterell, P. and Morris, C. (2012) 'The capacity, impact and challenge of service users experiential knowledge', in M. Barnes and P. Cotterell (eds) *Critical perspectives on user involvement*, Bristol: The Policy Press, pp 57–69.

Department of Health (1999) *National service framework for mental health: modern standards and service models*, London: Department of Health.

Evans, J., Rose, D., Flach, C., Csipke, E., Glossop, H., McCrone, P., Craig, T. and Wykes, T. (2012) 'Voice: developing a new measure of service users' perceptions of inpatient care, using a participatory methodology', *Journal of Mental Health*, vol 21, no 1, pp 57–71.

Faulkner, A. (2004) *The ethics of survivor research: guidelines for the ethical conduct of research carried out by mental health service users and survivors*, York: Joseph Rowntree Foundation.

Faulkner, A. (2010) *Changing our worlds: examples of user controlled research in action*, Eastleigh: INVOLVE.

Faulkner, A. and Layzell, S. (2000) *Strategies for living: a report of user-led research into people's strategies for living with mental distress*, London: The Mental Health Foundation.

Faulkner, A. and Nicholls, V. (1999) *The DIY guide to survivor research*, London: The Mental Health Foundation.

Glasby, J. and Beresford, P. (2006) 'Who knows best? Evidence-based practice and the service user contribution', *Critical Social Policy*, vol 26, no 1, pp 268–84.

Harding, S. (1987) *Feminism and methodology*, Buckingham: Open University Press.

Harding, S. (1993) 'Rethinking standpoint epistemology: "What is strong objectivity?"', in L. Alcoff and E. Potter (eds) *Feminist epistemologies*, London: Routledge, pp 49–82.

Harding, S. (1997) 'Comment on Hekman's "Truth and method: feminist standpoint revisited": whose standpoint needs the regimes of truth and reality?', *Signs: Journal of Women in Culture and Society*, vol 22, no 2, pp 383–91.

Hartsock, N. (1997) 'Comment on Hekman's "Truth and method: feminist standpoint theory revisited": truth or justice?', *Signs: Journal of Women in Culture and Society*, vol 22, no 2, pp 367–74.

Hekman, S. (1997) 'Truth and method: feminist standpoint theory revisited', *Signs: Journal of Women in Culture and Society*, vol 22, no 2, pp 341–65.

May, R. (2004) 'Making sense of psychotic experiences and working towards recovery', in J. Gleeson and P. McGorry (eds) *Psychological interventions in early psychosis*, New York, NY: John Wiley, pp 245–6.

Mercer, G. (2002) 'Emancipatory disability research', in C. Barnes, M. Oliver and L. Barton (eds) *Disability studies today*, Cambridge: Polity.

Nicholls, V. (2001) *Doing research ourselves*, London: Mental Health Foundation, Strategies For Living.

Oliver, M. (1990) *The politics of disablement*, Basingstoke: Macmillan.

Oliver, M. (1992) 'Changing the social relations of research production', *Disability, Handicap & Society*, vol 7, no 2, pp 101–14.

Oliver, M. (1996) *Understanding disability: from theory to practice*, Basingstoke: Macmillan.

Oliver, M. and Barnes, C. (2012) *The new politics of disablement*, Basingstoke: Palgrave/Macmillan.

Rose, D. (2009) 'Survivor produced knowledge', in A. Sweeney, P. Beresford, A. Faulkner, M. Nettle and D. Rose (eds) *This is survivor research*, Ross-on-Wye: PCSS Books, pp 38–43.

Rose, D., Wykes, T., Bindman, J. and Fleischmann, P. (2005) 'Information, consent and perceived coercion: consumers' views on ECT', *British Journal of Psychiatry*, vol 186, pp 54–9.

Rose, D., Wykes, T., Farrier, D., Dolan A.-M., Sporle, T. and Bogner, D. (2008) 'What do clients think of cognitive remediation therapy? A consumer-led investigation of satisfaction and side effects', *American Journal of Psychiatric Rehabilitation*, vol 11, no 2, pp 181–204.

Rose, D., Sweeney, A., Leese, M., Clement, S., Burns, T., Catty, J. and Wykes, T. (2009) 'Developing a user-generated measure of continuity of care: brief report', *Acta Psychiatrica Scandinavica*, vol 119, no 4, pp 320–4.

Rose, D., Leese, M., Oliver, D., Bennewith, O., Priebe, S. and Wykes, T. (2011a) 'A comparison of participant information elicited by service user and non-service user researchers', *Psychiatric Services*, vol 62, no 2, pp 210–213.

Rose, D., Evans, J., Sweeney, A. and Wykes, T. (2011b) 'A model for developing outcome measures from the perspectives of mental health service users', *International Review of Psychiatry*, vol 23, no 1, pp 41–6.

Simmons, R., Powell, M. and Greener, I. (eds) (2009) *The consumer in public services: choice, values and difference*, Bristol: The Policy Press.

Sweeney, A., Beresford, P., Faulkner, A., Nettle, M. and Rose, D. (eds) (2009) *This is survivor research*, Ross-on-Wye: PCSS Books.

Thomas, C. (2007) *Sociologies of disability and illness: contested ideas in disability studies and medical sociology*, Basingstoke: Palgrave Macmillan.

Thomas, G. and Loxley, A. (2001) *Deconstructing special education and constructing inclusion*, Buckingham: Open University Press.

Trivedi, P. (2009) 'Are we who we say we are – or who they think we are?', in J. Reynolds, R. Muston, T. Heller, J. Leach, M. McCormick, J. Wallcraft and M. Walsh (eds) *Mental health still matters*, Basingstoke: Palgrave, pp 224–7.

Turner, M. and Beresford, P. (2005) 'User Controlled Research: its meanings and potential', Eastleigh: INVOLVE.

humanity and personhood, and with the upholding of citizenship status and rights (Fraser, 2000; Lister, 2004, 2007).

Recognition politics are also concerned with exposing and challenging the symbolic operation of power. For Bourdieu (1992, p 170), power operates through the ways in which language and ideology come to construct social belief – the power of 'constituting the given'. He terms the wielding of symbolic power 'symbolic violence', a form of domination and oppression that comes from constructing reality in ways that privilege the knowledge and culture of the dominant group, and through practices of social exclusion and inferiorisation that may lead to 'internalised oppression'. It is resisted through symbolic struggle to assert alternative meanings and values that afford dominated individuals and groups a higher social status and worth.

What is key here, then, is that the importance of recognition is not just socio-political, but also personal, with a strong moral dimension to the issue (Honneth, 1995). Recognition denials can inflict harm and be personally damaging, undermining people's identities and self-worth; they can be a form of oppression (Taylor, 1992; Honneth, 1995; Lister, 2004; Lovell, 2007). Struggles for social recognition are thus also struggles for self-esteem (feeling valued by one's social groups and society as a whole), self-respect (a sense of moral and legal personhood and of 'the possession of universal human rights') and 'self-confidence' (emotional ontological security) (Honneth, 1995, p 119).

In the context of the politics of 'new social movements' and of citizenship, recognition has been sought for universal shared humanity and equal moral worth for those who are socially marginalised or subordinated (Honneth, 1995; Fraser, 1999, 2000; Lister, 2007), drawing on human rights principles such as respect and value for persons (Lister, 2004). It has also been sought for cultural identity and experience (Fraser, 2000; Honneth, 2003), as underpinned by human rights principles of autonomy (or self-determination) and dignity (Honneth, 1995; Dean, 2008). Both types of claim – universality and distinctiveness[3] – are interdependent with civil, political, social and economic rights. For instance, Fraser (2000) views the actualisation of full societal participation for subordinated groups as predicated upon their cultural revaluation, while Cresswell (2009) asserts that social and political rights are constituted by the assertion of 'experiential rights'. Similarly, Lister (2004) notes how socially derived respect and esteem are necessary for the full realisation of participation in public affairs, as a political right of citizenship (although she argues that the relationship here is in fact a dialectical one). Many theorists thus discuss cultural recognition, along with imbricated socio-economic 'redistribution' and political representation, as essential to the realisation of participatory parity in the public sphere (Honneth, 1995; Fraser, 1997, 2000, 2007; Fraser and Honneth, 2003; Lister, 2004; Lovell, 2007), although the nature and direction of these relationships remain disputed.

This chapter brings a range of recognition theories (see Lovell, 2007), as a perspective on human rights, to bear on the study of user involvement in mental health services. Its focus is on the construction of identity and experience through the discourses, structural organisation and relations of these services and user involvement, and how these relate to participation and equality.

## The study

The aim of the study was to explore the outcomes of user involvement policies for the participation of women and men service users within mental health services and for the development of these services. It was conducted in the north-east of Scotland, where various statutory- and voluntary-sector forums for user involvement had been established. The study involved three of these, sampled purposively according to their institutional affiliation and status: a statutory-sector service user group, a voluntary-sector community group (members of which included service practitioners and providers as well as users) and an independent mutual support group. The main purpose of the first group was to disseminate information and to act as a conduit for users' views, while the second group had a stronger lobbying function, and the third was primarily a support group.

The study was conducted from a feminist critical discourse-analytic perspective (Fairclough, 1992; Lazar, 2005), and so focused on the constitution of power in and through language and other elements of social interaction. It accommodated a twofold conception of discourse: as a way of understanding, or a set of ideas about, a particular phenomenon that works ideologically in conjunction with other elements of social practice (eg the discourse of 'mental illness') (Fairclough, 1992); and, since discourses are often associated with particular fields of social action and institutions and combine in particular ways, as 'knowledges' and the totality of interactions in a given field (eg 'psychiatric discourse') (Fairclough, 2001).

A collaborative, 'interactive' and action-oriented feminist methodological approach was adopted (see Lewis, 2007), while multiple, qualitative research methods were employed, including: participant observation at group meetings; interviews and informal interactions with service users (female, $n = 9$; male, $n = 16$), practitioners ($n = 2$) and providers/policymakers ($n = 3$); and policy analysis.[4] This chapter draws mainly upon the participant observation and service user interviews.

## User involvement as recognition politics

With the onset of user involvement, service users had become legitimate participants in the planning and development of mental health services in the locality. Motivated by a desire to help themselves and others, and with growing acceptance of their increasing role, their 'presence' and 'voice' were changing the cultural landscape of these services, and there were personal gains for them, described mainly in terms of mutual support and opportunities for expression. However, the policy initiative simultaneously produced various failures of recognition, which, in turn, worked to structure the social and political field of user involvement in mental health services in the locale. In achieving 'representation' for service users, then, user involvement had opened spaces within which recognition politics were played out (Fraser, 2007). In what follows, I discuss these politics in relation to non-recognition and disrespect, first, and then misrecognition and the discourse of mental illness.

## Non-recognition and disrespect: being a 'user'[5]

An intriguing finding of the study was how the policy discourse of user involvement itself had disempowering and derogatory effects and, as such, was itself contested by those taking part as service users. This was partly due to the 'involvement' element of the discourse working to delimit the degree of participation and influence afforded to service users. However, it was also because the discourses and practices of user involvement were centred around people *being* users of mental health services and categorising people according to their 'type of mental health problem' (see Lewis, 2005; Hui and Stickley, 2007). As the following participant notes, this meant that user involvement inevitably had reductionist, homogenising and pathologising effects through positioning people primarily in terms of their relationship to services (Beresford, 2000) and their concomitant 'mental illness':

> "Even in places like the [named group], people who go along to that, you go along as a service user, and even though it's not meant, with the best will in the world people see you as a service user, because you wouldn't be there unless you had a mental illness. So, even though they're trying to combat that, in a sense, what they're still seeing first is the

mental illness … [as opposed to] the woman or the man or
whatever; you know it seems to take centre stage." (Carol)[6]

So, as this participant observes, in the context of user involvement,
people became occluded from view by their 'mental illness' ascription,
and within the institutional confines of mental health services, it
seemed impossible to eschew or to ideologically de-invest the service
user identity (Fairclough, 1992). The discourse and practices of user
involvement consequently had their own marginalising and dominating
effects through objectification and dividing practices (Foucault, 1982),
which differentially marked 'users' from others in a hierarchical relation
(Williams, 1999) and work to 'split off' those seen as mentally ill 'from
the rest of humanity' (Pilgrim, 2008, p 302). This identity construction
resulted not only in status subordination and the undermining of full
societal membership for service users (Fraser, 2003), but also in a kind
of dehumanisation as people became denied 'wholeness' (Cresswell,
2009) and, thus, full humanity. As such, 'service users' were prevented
from participating in the (semi-)public arenas of user involvement
as fully fledged partners on the grounds of both inequality of social
standing (Fraser, 2003) and unequal endowment with the moral rights
of 'the person' (Honneth, 1995).

These findings demonstrate how official movements towards valuing
people and even attempts at universalist recognition can 'set in motion
a second – stigmatising – recognition dynamic' (Fraser, 1997, p 25).
The preceding participant's reflections reveal the way in which 'user
group' politics in health care have often centred upon 'claims for the
realization of personhood, for cultural respect, autonomy and dignity'
(Williams, 1999, p 673). Yet, the very political alignments of service user
groups themselves work to simplify and reify group identities (Fraser,
2000), which 'act back upon their incumbents' (Taylor, 1998, p 341) and
forestall mutual recognition (Crossley, 2004) and parity of participation
(Fraser, 2003). In the context of mental health services, these effects
are magnified by the stigmatising and all-defining nature of a 'mental
illness' identity, which it is impossible to positively assert (Hodge, 2005;
see also Lister, 2004). Thus, through encouraging segregation and
chauvinism, these dividing practices and resulting reification of 'mental
illness' identities not only 'risk sanctioning violations of human rights'
through constructing people as less than human, but also risk 'freezing
the very antagonisms … [they] purport to mediate' (Fraser, 2000, p 108).

Some participants reflected on the ideological and political effects
of the 'user' construct itself. One female respondent, for example,
commented, "most genuine people don't use, they contribute", thereby

indicating the ways in which the discourse constructed 'users' as deficient in certain respects (ie as failing to contribute) and therefore how it could work to undermine the value and efforts of individuals, positioning them as of unequal moral worth (Fraser, 1997). Another male interviewee pointed out its implication in constituting relations of dependency, as "a 'service user', it implies that you're addicted to them". Consequently, as another participant pointed out, "nobody wants to be called a user", and many participants resisted or refused the construction in favour of 'more respectable' alternatives, while the identity issues associated with taking part motivated some people to distance or dissociate themselves from user involvement activities.[7]

These findings illustrate again how welfare identity categories and official policies aimed at recognition can have unintended consequences, through which they produce their own injustices of recognition. They also illustrate how these identity categories have become a focus for resistance within the organising of many disability, service user and survivor groups, underpinned by demands for respect, autonomy and dignity (Williams, 1999). In the absence of a more fully developed and consensual social rights perspective in respect of welfare provision, the preceding participants were aware of how 'users' inevitably became 'construed as inadequate, blameworthy or undeserving', and that the construction of dependence was a means through which power was exercised (Hoggett, 2000, p 193) and was corrosive of citizenship rights (Lister, 2007). Moreover, these injustices of recognition could be highly personally damaging and distorting, reflecting back to people a 'confining ... demeaning ... and contemptible picture of themselves' (Taylor, 1992, p 25) and threatening their self-respect and self-esteem (Honneth, 1995).

The discourse and practices of user involvement thus had competing and contradictory effects; they opened up spaces in which such hierarchical social relations could be contested and distinctions redrawn (Williams, 1999) and in which a 'service user' identity provided legitimation for participation and some sense of being personally valued, but this identity simultaneously worked to dominate, segregate and inferiorise 'users' and to deny them equality and symbolic justice (Fraser, 2000, 2007; Lister, 2004). In addition, as the following participant points out, forms of misrecognition could be both a social barrier and a motivating force for those taking part (Honneth, 1995):

> "For a lot of us, it's been a hard struggle and a fight; we don't even believe in our own worth, to then start saying, 'Hey, I can probably teach other people things', whatever it is, you

know, total reversal of role, 'Oh yeah, I've got something to offer the world, I'm far from being a nobody.'" (Mark)

There was also the issue of the status of user groups in the field of mental health services and in wider society (see Honneth, 1995) and how this related to the achievement of participatory parity in user involvement activities (see Fraser, 2000, 2003; Lister, 2004). The following extract demonstrates the pain and anger that injuries of status inequality, inferiorisation and misrecognition could invoke (Honneth, 1995, 2003; Wilkinson, 2005), as well as Fraser's (2007, p 20) point that 'people can ... be prevented from interacting on terms of parity by institutionalized hierarchies of cultural value that deny them the requisite standing':

"You're classed as some sort of underdog, that's for sure ... you only have to mention 'user groups' and 'network groups' and 'empowerment groups' and anything voluntary. If you haven't got a paid job, haven't got a title, then you're the underdog. No matter how much you say you've got empowerment, you don't have it." (Barbara)

This quotation illustrates once more how user involvement, as a policy initiative, could have the effect of reproducing and reinforcing a low social status for participants, of reconstituting an inferior, devalued and marginalised position for 'mental health service users' (Williams, 1999; Fraser, 2000; Lister, 2007). Moreover, there could be practices of subjugation within the activities of user involvement themselves. Concurring with other research (eg Rutter et al, 2004), the accounts of statutory-sector service providers tended to infantilise and patronise service users (see Lewis, 2012), constructing them in subordinating terms that were often experienced as disparagement by service users, especially the men, one of whom commented:

"Really, you have to burrow your way in and, if necessary, put up with all kinds of people you don't like, and go along with practices you don't like, and swallow quite a lot of insults as well. The earliest phase, when we first set up the 50/50 partnership was that anything we put down on paper should be in simple language that the users could understand – because we're all supposed to be stupid, you know." (Steve)

This extract highlights yet again the competing and contradictory effects of practices in the area of user involvement, which could be aimed at affording people value through inclusiveness, but result in being 'insulting' to some. It illustrates an 'evaluative form of disrespect' or degradation in the sense of diminished social esteem or status, and how the sense of injustice this evokes can provide the moral imperative and motivation for struggles for recognition (Honneth, 1995, 2003).

Many participants engaged in forms of subversion and resistance to institutionalised relations and practices of social subordination (Fraser, 2000) while participating in user involvement activities. For instance, one described how he 'dressed up' for meetings ("a radical approach with a clean shirt on"), a kind of presentation of self (Goffman, 1959) viewed as a means of symbolically challenging the status service users were prescribed. Through such discursive practices, in recognising the operation of power, and through seeking to expose, understand and challenge this, participants were engaged in symbolic struggle – both personal and social (Bourdieu, 1992). Theirs was a struggle for recognition of power operating within and through ostensibly benign, helping relations and institutions, a form of political resistance dependent on moral insight into injustice (Honneth, 1995). As I now discuss, these recognition struggles inevitably included battles against the constitutive work of the discourse of mental illness.

## Misrecognition: the discourse of mental illness

While user involvement had (ostensibly) been established as an attempt to value service users' views and contributions, and some participants did describe deriving some personal value from taking part, their experiences were mainly described in terms of a sense of being devalued – or misrecognised – in the course of its activities. Indeed, in accordance with other research (eg Connor and Wilson, 2006), there were complaints from service users about not feeling 'listened to' at all levels of interaction with services. At the level of service planning and development, for example, in the context of the treatment of a report of a local user consultation exercise, participants often referred to the difficulty of being 'taken seriously'. Evidently being used to such inferiorisation, for the women service users, there was often a taken-for-grantedness about this, while two of the men participants explained the phenomenon as being due to a lack of institutional status and associated 'credibility', one pointing out that unlike that of many service users, my work had the benefit of 'academic respectability'. However, participants also implicated in this context matters of social identity in terms of (psychiatric) 'labelling', referring to the difficulty of asserting one's views, insofar as expressions of dissatisfaction, being upset, anger and so forth could become attributed to one's 'mental illness': "There's always, when you say something controversial, 'Oh well, she's not feeling very well at the moment' muttered under people's breath" (Carol); "I mean, you can just write off users' views, you know, 'Here he is being paranoid; here he is being depressed', you know, you can and that's it" (Chris).

These extracts evidence the insidious workings of power within the field of user involvement in mental health services, which worked through psychiatric constructions not only undermining the authority and credibility of service users' views, but also individualising and pathologising them. They illustrate the centrality of an 'illness' concept in producing these effects along with the ways in which moral legitimacy and the ascription of rights are undermined when people are deemed mad (Busfield, 2006; Cresswell, 2009; Spandler and Calton, 2009). Such discrediting and delegitimising, or 'psychiatric disqualification' (Lindow, 1991), can be understood as a form of symbolic violence towards service users who were battling for social recognition – of their views, their experiences and, indeed, ultimately their humanity (see Crossley, 2004). The compelling injustice of this misrecognition was noted by one participant in the context of discussing a long-standing dispute over the payment of his expenses for attending meetings: "I'm still the madman because I'm the one who's kicking up all this bloody fuss over £1.50" (Steve).

A related issue was the undermining of moral responsibility by psychiatric discourse. Steve insisted in the context of his interactions with services that little would be gained unless workers could "stop seeing people as sick people who can't be trusted". Justice was for him, then, a matter not only of being afforded value, dignity and respect, but also of being recognised as a responsible moral agent of full integrity and common humanity, of equal moral worth (Williams, 1999; Lister, 2007). The particular importance of this was illustrated by a female participant's account of the de-authorising effects of mental illness constructions on subjectivity "to the point where you can no longer trust your own judgement". Being denied universal recognition, being 'misrecognised', was consequently to risk suffering not only 'an injury to one's identity' but also 'a distortion of one's relation to one's self' (Fraser, 2000, p 109).

The ways in which psychiatric discourse could work to undermine service users' authority to speak and to act were thus displayed here. Furthermore, the research illustrated the particular violence created when psychiatric discourse rubs up against an understanding of user involvement as conditional upon the advanced liberal 'individualistic ethic of self-responsibility' (Dean, 2008, p 6). At one meeting, service users became castigated by a senior male psychiatrist for failing to take 'responsibility' for their own problems, while their 'dependency' became construed as behavioural, thereby serving to obscure the actual social construction of this dependency and struggles against this (Williams, 1999; see also Connor and Wilson, 2006). In this manner, the discourse of psychiatry served to legitimate a denial of the right to participation. The extreme injustice of this in the face of the New Labour policy mantra of interdependent 'rights and responsibilities' of citizenship (Williams, 1999; Dean, 2008) was particularly striking, since these areas of moral jurisdiction became mutually denied to users of mental health services.

The symbolic injustice of 'psychiatrising' as a form of misrecognition in all of these contexts was evident from, and indeed amplified by, its repressive effects. It worked to silence service users, especially the women, in the public and semi-public arenas of user involvement: one woman confided that it had led her to decide against raising an issue at a meeting, while a male participant described how awareness of the matter among service users meant that he was one of the few prepared to speak out, even though the consequent 'stress' of this could have deleterious effects on his own mental health. It also tied to a great deal of suppression of criticism in user involvement fora and in the formal interviews for this research – something attributed by one woman participant to a "lack of self-esteem". Furthermore, among the women, this suppression sometimes encompassed self-blame for problems experienced in interactions with services, and this seemed to be exacerbated by the effects of psychiatric discourse in personalising socially generated phenomena.

Along with forms of non-recognition and disrespect, then, misrecognition as a result of the dominating effects of psychiatric discourse, and the discourse of mental illness in particular, also served to impede parity of participation in mental health service planning and policymaking for service users and thus to deny them full access in practice to their right to participation in this context (Honneth, 1995; Fraser, 2000, 2003; Lister, 2004).

## Conclusion

This study conducted in one UK locality demonstrated how, while the official aim of user involvement to afford value to service users and their views in order to promote service improvement and democratisation had been partially achieved, recognition for service users was forestalled by the discourse and practices of user involvement, as tied to the discourse of mental illness and other elements of the wider discourse of psychiatry. Indeed, they simultaneously reconstituted a two-dimensional failure of recognition for service users: status subordination (Fraser, 2000) and psychiatric disqualification (Lindow, 1991; Crossley, 2004). Service users were therefore denied an equal voice, full humanity and equal moral worth (see Honneth, 1995; Fraser, 2000, 2003; Lister, 2004) and these recognition denials were the focus of their symbolic struggle (Bourdieu, 1992; see also Williams, 1999). As such, the current social and cultural framework of user involvement in mental health services and the incumbent systematic failure to recognise users' views and experiences, discussed by way of introduction and further evidenced by this research, amounts to a dereliction of the core principles underlying human rights – dignity, equality, respect, fairness and autonomy – principles that have been proclaimed as the value base for health care (DH, 2007).

This failure to achieve participatory parity for service users and associated rights violations are institutional harms that require institutional remedies at the level of mental health policy and services (Fraser, 2000). This study indicates that this institutional change needs to be two-pronged to address matters of both status and identity, and both structural and cultural in focus (Fraser, 1997).

First, since different valuations are underpinned by discourses (Fairclough, 1992; Lister, 2007), there is a need to rebalance mental health policy and services away from individualised and medicalised understandings of distress and associated responses, and towards a social model and community development approach built on humanistic principles and centred around people's social locations and associated life experiences (see, eg, Coppock and Hopton, 2000; Tew, 2005). This would help destabilise 'mental illness' dichotomies and counter the dominating effects of psychiatric discourse that currently comes largely from the taken-for-grantedness of its schemas (Bourdieu, 1992). It would ensure that people seeking help to overcome distress were afforded both social recognition (full societal membership) and universalist recognition (full humanity) (Fraser, 1999, 2003), working to unburden those in this position of 'excessive ascribed or constructed distinctiveness' (Fraser, 2000, p 115), of stigma.

Current policy in the UK is providing potential for some positive strategic development in this direction. In England, we are witnessing radical changes in the arrangements for commissioning and delivering mental health services, with a stronger role to be played by primary care and local authorities (see HMG and DH, 2011; Joint Commissioning Panel for Mental Health, 2012). Local councils are taking on public health responsibilities, with mental health viewed as integral and a priority, and are developing Health and Wellbeing Boards which will oversee and scrutinise Local Clinical Commissioning Groups. These changes may enhance possibilities for greater movement towards unmedicalised, community-based mental health services provision (see Centre for Mental Health et al, 2012). Similarly, there are promising policy developments in Scotland concerning assets-based approaches, community empowerment and renewal and the integration of health and social care (Mulvagh, 2012). However, there is still a need for an expansion of cultural agency and of discursive contestation (Fraser, 1997; Lister, 2007) within debates about mental health policy and services, including on the part of service user groups, to ensure that we all start thinking in more social and politicised terms about mental distress (see Lewis, 2009). Achieving this requires further reframing of this political arena. Currently, user involvement suffers a political injustice of misrepresentation not only in terms of unequal participation for service users, but also in terms of misframing (Fraser, 2007), as 'mental health service users' have become the containers for fears about 'mental illness' (Hoggett, 2000). To redress this, any public engagement strategy for mental health should be informed by a 'politics of differentiated universalism' (Lister, 1997) that recognises common humanity, citizenship and equal worth as well as the social inequalities and exclusions that frame people's lives (Williams, 1999; Lister, 2007). There is a need to engage public concern through statutory participation mechanisms (such as Public Partnership Forums in Scotland) and a wide range of stakeholder organisations and groups within and beyond the field of mental health, including those of service users/survivors and women, thereby highlighting the connection of mental health to social/political action in other fields (Lewis, 2009).

Second, there is a need to outwardly challenge the current hierarchical relations that characterise mental health services and to work towards recognition of the status of service users as full partners at all levels of interaction (see Fraser, 2000, 2001; Lister, 2004). This will require a recasting of current 'user involvement' policies and practices to ensure that these explicitly address institutionalised power and inequality within mental health services (see Stickley, 2006). A core aim here is to change 'institutionalized patterns of cultural value' that impede equal participation in decision-making (Fraser, 2003, p 218), something that also requires a rebalancing of economic rewards for contributions

(Honneth, 1995). At the policymaking level, one effective approach is that of 'co-governance', which officially recognises the authority and legitimacy of democratic, self-governing advocacy organisations in the policy process, with their representatives 'participat[ing] in at least two arenas – that of their own movement and that of established power ... draw[ing] their strength and autonomy from their own organizations' (Bochel et al, 2007, p 208). In the case of mental health, this would include service user/survivor organisations and others based around experiences of oppression.

Taken together, these measures can help realise the currently unfulfilled recognition aims of user involvement and concomitant human rights principles for health care in the context of mental health, and, indeed, help safeguard the human rights of us all.

## Acknowledgements

This work draws upon material from Lydia Lewis (2009) 'Politics of recognition: what can a human rights perspective contribute to understanding users' experiences of involvement in mental health services?', *Social Policy and Society*, vol 8, no 2, pp 257–74 (© Cambridge University Press, reproduced with permission).

This chapter is dedicated to the memory of Ross Graham, who fought for symbolic justice in the field of mental health services. I would like to thank all those who participated in this study and the reviewers of this chapter and the original article. The study was funded by the Medical Research Council (MRC) and the writing of the article upon which this chapter is based by an Economic and Social Research Council/MRC Post-Doctoral Fellowship.

## Notes

[1] These terms indicate differing identities, with the term 'survivor' used to denote survival of both distress and service usage, and 'service user' being less political.

[2] The New Labour government was in power at the time the research reported in this chapter was conducted and the article it is based on was written.

[3] In the mental health field, these two approaches have sometimes been described as 'normalisation' versus celebrating difference ('madness').

[4] Ethical permissions were gained from the regional Research Ethics Committee.

[5] For stylistic reasons only, inverted comments are not always used when referring to 'users' or 'service users'.

[6] Participants have been given pseudonyms. Transcribing conventions: '...' indicates missing speech; and square brackets, added text or text changed for anonymity.

[7] Note here the importance of context for the political and ideological investments of types of discourse (Fairclough, 1992), since such stigmatising effects do not necessarily arise from being a 'service user' in other settings.

## References

Beresford, P. (2000) 'Service users' knowledges and social work theory: conflict or collaboration?', *British Journal of Social Work*, vol 30, pp 489–503.

Bochel, C., Bochel, H., Somerville, P. and Worley, C. (2007) 'Marginalised or enabled voices? "User participation" in policy and practice', *Social Policy and Society*, vol 7, no 2, pp 201–10.

Bourdieu, P. (1992) *Language and symbolic power*, Cambridge: Polity Press.

Busfield, J. (2006) 'Mental disorder and human rights', in L. Morris (ed) *Rights: sociological perspectives*, London and New York, NY: Routledge.

Campbell, P. (2006) 'Changing the mental health system – a survivor's view', *Journal of Psychiatric and Mental Health Nursing*, vol 13, pp 578–80.

Carr, S. (2007) 'Participation, power, conflict and change: theorising dynamics of service user participation in the social care system of England and Wales', *Critical Social Policy*, vol 27, no 2, pp 266–76.

Centre for Mental Health, Department of Health, Mind, NHS Confederation Mental Health Network, Rethink Mental Illness and Turning Point (2012) *No health without mental health: implementation framework*, London: Mental Health Strategy Branch.

Connor, S.L. and Wilson, R. (2006) 'It's important that they learn from us for mental health to progress', *Journal of Mental Health*, vol 15, no 4, pp 461–74.

Coppock, V. and Hopton, J. (2000) *Critical perspectives on mental health*, London: Routledge.

Cresswell, M. (2009) 'Psychiatric survivors and "experiential rights"', *Social Policy and Society*, vol 8, no 2, pp 231–43.

Crossley, N. (2004) 'Not being mentally ill: social movements, system survivors and the oppositional habitus', *Anthropology and Medicine*, vol 11, no 2, pp 161–80.

Dean, H. (2008) 'Social policy and human rights: re-thinking the engagement', *Social Policy and Society*, vol 7, no 1, pp 1–12.

DH (Department of Health) (2007) *Human rights in healthcare: a framework for local action*, London: Department of Health.

Fairclough, N. (1992) *Discourse and social change*, Cambridge: Polity Press.

Fairclough, N. (2001) 'The discourse of New Labour: critical discourse analysis', in M. Wetherell, A. Taylor and S. Yates (eds) *Discourse as data: a guide for analysis*, London: Sage.

Forbes, J. and Sashidharan, S.P. (1997) 'User involvement in services – incorporation or challenge?', *British Journal of Social Work*, vol 27, pp 481–98.

Foucault, M. (1982) 'The subject and power', *Critical Inquiry*, vol 8, pp 777–95.

Fraser, N. (1997) *Justice interruptus: critical reflections on the 'postsocialist' condition*, London: Routledge.

Fraser, N. (1999) 'Social justice in the age of identity politics: redistribution, recognition and participation', in L. Ray and A. Sayer (eds) *Culture and economy after the cultural turn*, London: Sage.

Fraser, N. (2000) 'Rethinking recognition', *New Left Review*, vol 3, pp 107–20.

Fraser, N. (2001) 'Recognition without ethics', *Theory, Culture and Society*, vol 18, nos 2/3, pp 21–42.

Fraser, N. (2003) 'Distorted beyond all recognition: a rejoinder to Axel Honneth', in N. Fraser and A. Honneth (eds) *Redistribution or recognition? A political–philosophical exchange*, London: Verso.

Fraser, N. (2007) 'Reframing justice in a globalising world', in T. Lovell (ed) *(Mis)Recognition, social inequality and social justice: Nancy Fraser and Pierre Bourdieu*, London: Routledge.

Fraser, N. and Honneth, A. (2003) *Redistribution or recognition? A political–philosophical exchange*, London: Verso.

Goffman, E. (1959) *Presentation of self in everyday life*, New York, NY: Doubleday.

HMG (Her Majesty's Government) and DH (Department of Health) (2011) *No health without mental health: a cross-government mental health outcomes strategy for people of all ages*, London: Department of Health.

Hodge, S. (2005) 'Participation, discourse and power: a case study in service user involvement', *Critical Social Policy*, vol 25, no 2, pp 164–79.

Hoggett, P. (2000) *Emotional life and the politics of welfare*, Basingstoke and London: Macmillan Press.

Honneth, A. (1995) *The struggle for recognition: the moral grammar of social conflicts* (trans J. Andersen), Cambridge: Polity Press.

Honneth, A. (2003) 'Redistribution as recognition', in N. Fraser and A. Honneth (eds) *Redistribution or recognition? A political–philosophical exchange*, London: Verso.

Hui, A. and Stickley, T. (2007) 'Mental health policy and mental health service user perspectives on involvement: a discourse analysis', *Journal of Advanced Nursing*, vol 59, no 4, pp 416–26.

Joint Commissioning Panel for Mental Health (2012) Briefing, London: Royal College of Psychiatrists. Available at: http://www.jcpmh.info/about/jcpmh-briefing/

Lazar, M. (2005) *Feminist critical discourse analysis: gender, power and ideology in discourse*, Basingstoke: Palgrave Macmillan.

Lewis, L. (2005) 'User involvement within Scottish mental health policy: locating power and inequality', *Scottish Affairs*, vol 51, pp 79–107.

Lewis, L. (2007) 'Epistemic authority and the gender lens', *The Sociological Review*, vol 55, no 2, pp 273–92.

Lewis, L. (2009) 'Mental health and human rights: a common agenda for user/survivor and women's groups?', *Policy & Politics*, vol 37, no 1, pp 75–92.

Lewis, L. (2012) '"It's people's whole lives": gender, class and the emotion work of user involvement in mental health services', *Gender, Work and Organisation,* vol 19, no 3, pp 276–305.

Lindow, V. (1991) 'Experts, lies and stereotypes', *The Health Service Journal*, August, pp 18–19.

Lister, R. (1997) *Citizenship: feminist perspectives*, Basingstoke: Palgrave Macmillan.

Lister, R. (2004) 'A politics of recognition and respect: involving people with experience of poverty in decision-making that affects their lives', in J. Andersen and B. Sim (eds) *The politics of inclusion and empowerment*, Hampshire: Palgrave Macmillan.

Lister, R. (2007) '(Mis)Recognition, social inequality and social justice: a critical social policy perspective', in T. Lovell (ed) *(Mis)Recognition, social inequality and social justice: Nancy Fraser and Pierre Bourdieu*, London: Routledge.

Lovell, T. (ed) (2007) *(Mis)Recognition, social inequality and social justice: Nancy Fraser and Pierre Bourdieu*, London: Routledge.

Mulvagh, L. (2012) 'Recovery and the assets-based approach', *Scottish Recovery Network Newsletter*, 18 July.

Parker, C. (2007) 'Developing mental health policy: a human rights perspective', in M. Knapp, D. McDaid, E. Mossialos and G. Thornicroft (eds) *Mental health policy and practice across Europe*, Oxford: Oxford University Press.

Pilgrim, D. (2008) '"Recovery" and current mental health policy', *Chronic Illness*, vol 4, no 4, pp 295–304.

Rutter, D., Manley, C., Weaver, T., Crawford, M. and Fulop, N. (2004) 'Patients or partners? Case studies of user involvement in the planning and delivery of adult mental health services in London', *Social Science and Medicine*, vol 58, pp 1973–84.

Shakespeare, T. (2005) 'Disabling politics? Beyond identity', *Soundings*, vol 30, pp 156–60.

Spandler, H. and Calton, T. (2009) 'Psychosis and human rights: conflicts in mental health policy and practice', *Social Policy and Society*, vol 8, no 2, pp 245–56.

Stickley, T. (2006) 'Should service user involvement be consigned to history? A critical realist perspective', *Journal of Psychiatric and Mental Health Nursing*, vol 13, pp 570–7.

Taylor, C. (1992) 'The politics of recognition', in C. Taylor and A. Gutmann (eds) *Multi-culturalism and 'the politics of recognition'*, Princeton, NJ: Princeton University Press.

Taylor, D. (1998) 'Social identity and social policy: engagements with postmodern theory', *Journal of Social Policy*, vol 27, no 3, pp 329–50.

Tew, J. (ed) (2005) *Social perspectives in mental health*, Philadelphia, PA: Jessica Kingsley Publishers.

Wilkinson, I. (2005) *The impact of inequality*, London and New York, NY: Routledge.

Williams, F. (1999) 'Good enough principles for welfare', *Journal of Social Policy*, vol 28, no 4, pp 667–87.

EIGHT

# Theorising a social model of 'alcoholism': service users who misbehave

*Patsy Staddon*

## Introduction

Service user involvement in research is by its nature political, in that it is aiming to effect change and improvement (McLaughlin, 2011). This is even more the case when service users disagree with established views as to what constitutes 'health' and 'normality' as regards their particular condition. Survivors of mental health treatment testify in this volume and elsewhere (Sweeney et al, 2009) to the fallibility and inadequacy of medical diagnoses and solutions (Rose, 2001). Survivors of alcohol and drug treatment have yet to develop their critical and political voice. This chapter considers some of the issues involved.

Faced with the damaging psychosocial consequences of extensive alcohol use, which are likely to include diminished personal esteem, loss of family support, loss of income and, ultimately, homelessness, alcohol service users tend to accept with little question a view of themselves as simultaneously immoral and ill. Mutual aid experts and academics support both positions:

> [We believe] that we are alcoholic and cannot manage our own lives.... That no human power could have relieved our alcoholism. (Alcoholics Anonymous, 1976, p 60)

> It is now admitted that the brain of an addicted patient no longer functions like a normal brain: it has lost the freedom to decide when confronted with the object of its addiction. (Reynaud, 2007, p 1513)

Most people who are or were 'alcoholics' appear to agree. They are likely to have learnt to talk about 'becoming sober', 'being in lifelong recovery'. They will try to do without the very substance that, like prescribed medication for other conditions, often enabled them to take part in that society, at least for some of the time (Ettorre, 2007). They may struggle desperately for approval from family and friends. The general acceptance of a moral ingredient to the condition skews research into its causes, affecting researcher, researched and public alike, telling us most about the society that has promoted it.

It was my ongoing distress as a recovered 'alcoholic', aware of the lifelong damage caused to my family and to me by this approach, which led me to examine the social injustice and oppression involved. After looking at all the issues for some time, from my perspective as a service user, I came to the conclusion that the principal beneficiaries are various commercial interests, those in positions of power, those employed in the treatment system and certain religious and moral groups, a view endorsed by Hammersley and Reid (2002). The losers are service users and their families.

My political will to change this situation drives this chapter's aim of theorising a social, as opposed to a medical, model of (particularly) women's alcohol 'misuse', which abuses those with a variety of social problems, mental health issues, low self-esteem and inadequate emotional support.

## The importance of alcohol

Anthropologists have noted the role of alcohol, across all cultures, in the attaining of time out and leisure (Eber, 2000 [1995]). It offers us the chance 'to explore aspects of ... life and processes of political and legal change, which are concerns of sociologists' (Gusfield, 1996, pp 5–6). It enables us to move away temporarily from distress, from normal social expectations and from 'self-imprisonment' (Gusfield, 1996, p 72). It may be a way of acting out, recreation, even a form of selfhood to which one has a right (Cresswell, 2009).

Alcohol is key to various spheres of adulthood and competence (Sulkunen, 2007). It may facilitate the virtual negation of social mores, while remaining firmly tied to the society in question (Stein, 1985). Used in this way, it could be said to occupy the space previously occupied by the carnival, the place of transgression on the borders of society (Presdee, 2000). The locale of the drinking, that is, its public nature, has also been seen as significant; as has the way that this has been understood by the public and by academics (Valentine et al, 2008). Alcohol use becomes problematic when the person or the person's social milieu decides that their life, or that of others, is being damaged in a way that is seen to be unacceptable.

## Alcohol use by women

There has been an increasing insistence by younger women on their right to drink and binge, in a way that has usually been seen as unexceptional for young men (Van Wersch and Walker, 2009). This is not usually drinking to drown sorrows, but to celebrate and to have fun. Often, it is not so much the substance in itself that is sought as much as the planning, the experience and the drama. Such drinking may be seen as a cultural challenge, allied with feminism (Thom, 1997).

Women may often invoke 'carnival' with the help of alcohol, accessing different behaviours as an essential 'other side' to their workaday selves:

> Having a laugh … fun … I liked it. I worked double day shifts; all the people were round about my age, or younger, and we used to go out like and take a few drugs and go round the pubs … it was fun … we had laughs together. ('Fran',[1] in Staddon, 2005b)

> [My dead husband] loved his drink … and about five or six times a year we all used to go out on a big bender, me included…. [My kids] would know when it was going to happen and they'd have a bucket ready for when I came in! They got quite practised at this! ('Ursula', in Staddon, 2005b)

> It didn't occur to me that there might be any problems at all at that time. It's just how I'd been growing up; it was the norm in life. You get drunk, you don't know what's happening, you wake up with some strange face in the bedroom. ('Bella', in Staddon, 2005b)

The increased popularity of the 'hen party', or 'girls' night out', is seen by some as a sign of women's greater freedom: 'different practices of drinking and belonging within late-night culture are being developed, and which should transform how we perceive women's role in engaging with alcohol and public space at night' (Eldridge and Roberts, 2008, p 326).

These nights out are watched by the rest of the world with a variety of emotions, including vicarious pleasure, since these freedoms have not traditionally been available to women. This is particularly marked when the activities border on the grotesque, challenging everyday notions of what is appropriate behaviour. It may be achieved by the use of more profane and noisy language than usual (Bakhtin, 1984 [1965]), or by spectacles such as women urinating in the street. Relaxing of concern for 'good behaviour' is often demonstrated in drunkenness, but 'It is the fact that culture continually challenges, disrupts and carnivalises the serious business of "order" that in itself becomes a threat to law and order' (Presdee, 2000, p 19).

## Alcohol and disorder

Carnival and excess have also been linked to a rejection of increasing rationalisation of everyday life, and a way of coping with community fragmentation (South, 1999). South also refers to society's needing to construct deviants, whereby substances make ideal social enemies for 'societies uncertain about their moral and constitutional strengths in other areas of life' (South, 1999, p 10). Alcohol may assist transgression and carnival, acting as a necessary flip side to order, one of community's functions. Without alcohol, it is harder for more constrained groups to take part, and groups with an essential caring function are least likely to be allowed to do so.

There is greater mainstream acceptability of deviant behaviour by wealthy, upper-class people and some celebrities. They are also part of a show, an entertainment for the rest of us (Veblen, 1994 [1897]; Mills, 2000 [1967]). The behaviour is still perceived as deviant; merely acceptably deviant for certain people at certain times. This enactment again connects with the functions of carnival and of ritual (Stein, 1985; Presdee, 2000). It does not include a general view that drunkenness, or madness, are valid ways of experiencing the world most of the time, and only exceptionally includes women's drunkenness at all. Fury is expressed when women in particular take these liberties as 'binge drinkers' and are seen to be 'out of control'.

Women are expected to take responsibility for moral order, while being denied full human rights (Coward, 1983; Lewis, 2009). This has often resulted in inequality and oppression, paradoxically leading women to use alcohol in ways that they may acknowledge to be harmful. They may be more likely to need 'time out', since they do more work over longer periods for less reward and their needs are likely to be spiritual and emotional as well as mental and physical (Ettorre and Riska, 1995). It is also easier for many women, in a society that prefers them, publicly at least, to demonstrate decorum, to express their sexuality when drunk (Traeen and Kvalem, 1996; Wilsnack and Beckman, 1984).

Unfortunately, whatever 'free choices' women may make, they lay themselves open to criticism in a way that men do not, since 'most discourses construct femininity in negative terms relative to masculinity' (Bowie, 2006 [2000], p 100). Concern is frequently expressed about their health, with particular anxiety about their function as future or current mothers. However, what seems principally at issue is their *right* to intoxication, indiscretion and inappropriate behaviour (Ettorre, 2007).

## The concept of 'alcoholism'

The use of alcohol, or any other substance, will be affected by changing social expectations and perceptions (Winlow, 2007), and this will apply to quantities consumed as well as what is acceptable by particular groups at particular times. There are precise and differing rules for each group in all societies (Goffman, 1971 [1959]). When someone is perceived to drink in a way that challenges expectations as to what is appropriate for them, with regard to their gender, age and social position, they will be stigmatised and punished. They have broken the rules.

The point at which our society came to develop the concept of heavy drinking as a problem, or as 'alcoholism', may have come with a wider availability of stronger substances as a part of the process of industrialisation. It became more respectable and morally superior, among the lower and middle classes, to be teetotal (Nicholls, 2009). At the same time, developing notions of 'psychosis' facilitated the view that those who were habitually drunk were affected by a disease from which there was no escape: addiction (McDonald, 1994). It has been claimed that society may be anxious to increase the regulation of lifestyles it sees as unhealthy because it feels a general lack of moral authority, previously offered by the nation state (Sulkunen, 2007). 'Alcoholism' can thus be seen as itself a social construct, serving numerous purposes that have less to do with health than with social control.

## Illness as social dissonance

There is a history of mental illness being understood as misbehaviour (Chesler, 1997 [1972]), and being treated with amusement, embarrassment, anger and disgust. People fear unexpected behaviour and responses, experiencing the uncomfortable sensation of being suddenly unsure of how to act themselves (Goffman, 1971 [1959]).

Szasz (1997) is one of many psychiatrists who have observed that 'insanity' has been used as a way of supporting the concept that such unwanted (mis)behaviours are diseases. They were thus made treatable by diagnosis and pharmacological intervention. Whatever the success or otherwise of such interventions, the political impetus is the restoration and maintenance of order and balance, in a society that risks becoming bland and meaningless (Huxley, 1932). An element of disorder is integral to the human experience, as is an awareness that our understanding of what constitutes 'order' and 'normality' are continually in evolution (Kuhn, 1970 [1962]).

Alcohol treatment is certainly based on an understanding of drunkenness as disorder. Its reflection of the commonplace understanding of alcoholism as misbehaviour (Campbell, 2000) may make recovery difficult, causing additional pain, guilt and stigma (Angove and Fothergill, 2003). This 'disease concept' involves an antithetical belief in a lifelong character flaw (Kurtz, 1991), which is nevertheless a 'disease'. Alcoholism as 'disease' attains 'a biological entity', muddling 'social discourse, moral dilemmas, psychological states and pharmacology' (Hammersley and Reid, 2002, p 8).

Overdrinking is seen as greedy and irresponsible not just by lay people, but also by many doctors. They may feel demoralised and even demeaned by these 'dirty work patients' (Shaw, 2004), or 'heart–sink patients'. A 2010 survey found that GPs 'had less motivation and task-related self-esteem for this work [and] derived little satisfaction from this work'. In consequence, they often failed to take up chances of further training in this area (Alcohol Research UK, 2010). These attitudes may be developed in clinical training, which includes informal elements likely to encourage them (Reilly, 2007, p 705). Trainee doctors may be exposed to 'enculturation', a 'hidden curriculum' of neutralising the emotions, promoting professional identity by an unofficial prospectus including humiliation and haphazard tuition (Lempp and Seele, 2004, p 771). Psychiatrists and GPs may well try to avoid treating patients for whom they have some sort of distaste based on 'moral grounds' (Deehan et al, 1998).

'Alcoholism' is therefore the source and the target of both blame and shame, particularly for women, whose behaviour is subject to more severe scrutiny, partly because of their iconic role in society (Fillmore, 1984). Women who drink in a way that is seen negatively put 'their femininity and female roles in society at risk … women who do drink too much are saying a big "no" to society. They do that unacceptable thing: lose control' (Ettorre, 1997, p 15).

Women are also seen as family anchor, central to upholding moral beliefs and maintaining social control, powerfully conjoining affection and responsibility (Coleman, 1988). Much academic literature describes the harm done to families by the alcohol use of partners and parents (Velleman and Templeton, 2007). Although there is also ample evidence that such family structures can be harmful to women and children (Dobash and Dobash, 1980; Itzin, 2000), there is little approval for mothers and daughters who reject them, particularly if they are using alcohol (Wilsnack and Beckman, 1984; Plant, 1997; Raine, 2001; Staddon, 2005a).

Their recovery also has most to do with non-treatment factors (Willenbring, 2010), with individual context being a crucial consideration (Lushin and Anastas, 2011). Most treatment centres, however, still include and promote an approach that presents alcoholism as a disease of the will: one is both immoral and ill (Perryman et al, 2011). This concept is partly based on research that has been done on people already in, or only recently released from, such treatment (Willenbring, 2010). Yet, such people are not typical of those with alcohol issues, most of whom do not present for alcohol treatment at all (Moss et al, 2007). It is significant that most people with alcohol problems recover without treatment due to changes in the life course, but this is not greatly publicised (Raistrick et al, 2006; Penberthy, 2007; Willenbring, 2010).

These factors help to explain that although important research shows that most kinds of alcohol treatment may be no more effective than no treatment at all (Project MATCH Research Group, 1997; UKATT, 2005), we see unceasing efforts by the government and health industry to get more and more service users into treatment, offering an impression of a problem under effective control.

## A sociological gaze

In contrast to this 'disease' approach, a social model of alcohol use would see alcohol as potentially helping people to deal with a variety of social issues, some of which might become more problematic either with or without its use. Alcohol could also facilitate behaviour that while unacceptable to some people for some of the time, is part of the construction of a complex and changing society and the mental well-being of many of its members. For some women, intoxication might be a need, and some would say, a right, encompassing leisure, risk and independence (Lupton, 1999; Eber, 2000 [1995]). This is an alternative, competing discourse to that of social causation or of personal inadequacy and 'addiction'. It suggests a considerable degree of interaction between the individual and society, with both changing over time in how they affect each other (Blumer, 1969).

To develop an alternative, social model of alcohol use, it is helpful first to consider the social models of disability (Oliver, 1998) and of mental health (Beresford, 2002). Oliver (1998) sees social oppression as being intrinsic to positivist models of disability, whereby the person is 'sick' and needs a 'cure' to become 'normal'. Disability may be understood in different ways in different societies, and be experienced differently by different income groups. It may become a commodity, providing an income for service industries, but its cause is seldom addressed.

Beresford (2002) develops the concept significantly. Pointing out the massive credibility of the condition called 'mental illness', even among service users, who have known no other framework, he shows how the concept is a construction with no sound basis, a 'deficit model':

> 'Mental illness' constitutes a medicalised individualised interpretation of the phenomenon it seeks to explain, describe and deal with. It is based on a deficit model, which presumes the pathology and inadequacy of 'the mentally ill' and which conceptualises their thoughts, emotions, perceptions and behaviours as wrong and defective. (Beresford, 2002, p 582)

Attempting to challenge this model may itself be seen as evidence of irrationality, as yet more evidence of deviance. Mental health goals of 'recovery' and 'cure' may not fit with the experience and needs of the service user. Practical aids and flexible personal support may be of greater value.

As pointed out earlier, most people do change destructive alcohol use on their own, over time, without recourse to treatment or mutual aid groups (Willenbring, 2010), but as long as most treatment in the UK is still presenting heavy alcohol use as a shaming and lifelong illness (Perryman et al, 2011), the lives of women who drink for pleasure, self-medication or relief from stress will be overshadowed and under threat. Social solutions are possible for 'treating' socially constructed 'diseases' (see the following section).

A social model of alcohol use includes an understanding of what makes alcohol attractive, and even necessary, particularly to marginalised groups. For women, these will, for example, commonly include previous experience of sexual abuse, domestic abuse, loneliness, depression and rage (Staddon, 2009). Treatment that ignores such issues, relying instead on a 'disease' terminology, makes acknowledging these experiences difficult, with grief being seen as self-pity and 'seeking an excuse to drink' (Hausmann et al, 2008). The situation is not improved by some overworked GPs: 'I deal with what comes up ... except generally asking people their level of alcohol ... we don't go out looking for the problem. We've got enough to do with everything else!' (GP, cited in Staddon, 2009).

## Accommodating difference

A more flexible approach to alcohol would need a considerable shift in popular, medical and judicial views as to the appropriate behaviour and responsibilities of women and the nature of 'health'. However, such a cultural change might be to the advantage of many less powerful social groups. Greater respect for holistic well-being, and the right to control over one's own body, might lessen the need to use alcohol to make everyday life experience bearable and even pleasurable. This respect would include an acknowledgement of equal rights to pleasure, relaxation, sexuality and spirituality. The right to experience alternative ways of being and of living is one for which people have struggled throughout history.

A social model of alcohol use would help considerably with such an aim. It might:

- offer more diverse and accessible support, particularly for women who use alcohol and for staff who may find themselves working with them; and
- promote an acceptance that alcohol use is an inevitable outcome of inequalities of all description.

An investigation of the first of these changes is currently being undertaken in a service user-controlled research pilot beginning in Devon and Cornwall in June 2012.[2] Service user control over its process should produce some new and exciting ideas for the future of women's alcohol needs. That this can happen was evidenced by the success of Women's Independent Alcohol Support (WIAS), the service user-controlled social and support group that developed from my PhD work and ran for four further years.

The second change would require a wider understanding of the role of inequality in a variety of social ills; that is, 'structural violence' (Wilkinson and Pickett, 2009, p 134). One example of this would be to focus on the different ways that women still feel that their lives are controlled, such as by destructive relationships, lower income, poorer diet, the demands of fashion, less time in education, greater family commitments and the effects these have on women's health. This could lead to exploring the cultural changes whereby women's alcohol use may come to be seen less as a misfortune and more as a demand for equality. This is a change that will take some time to achieve, but can be addressed politically and personally.

## Conclusion

It is discouraging to view any condition as chronic and relapsing, as alcoholism is currently and inaccurately understood (Cunningham and McCambridge, 2012). If a social model of alcohol use were adopted, GPs and others might feel less critical and helpless and more motivated to help with those aspects of alcohol use that did find their way to the surgery. A new kind of support service might evolve, with the many different aspects of life that induce people to take refuge in alcohol being addressed in ways that did not place the blame for misfortune upon its recipients. This service could include ways of supporting families when parents and carers need time out, seeing this as part of a person's social and spiritual needs, and thus removing shame and stigma.

It is true that the odds are stacked against this. Alcohol service users and their families and friends do not yet possess the degree of empowerment to be seen among mental health survivors. Neither are they particularly welcome among those survivors, who may see their own legitimacy threatened by the inclusion of a more disreputable company, even when the needs of the two groups so frequently overlap. As many as two thirds of women with substance misuse issues may be suffering from additional mental health disorders (Zilberman et al, 2003) and might be considered to be using the alcohol for purposes of self-medication.

It is one thing to develop a social model of alcohol use, but quite another to convince alcohol survivors of their own self-worth and their right to appropriate support and social acceptance. However, it is a necessary first step.

### Notes
[1] Participants have been given pseudonyms. Transcribing conventions: '…' indicates missing speech; and square brackets, added text or text changed for anonymity.

² 'In what ways might the support needs of women with alcohol issues be improved? A qualitative research study using telephone interviews' (Staddon, University of Plymouth, 2012–13).

## References

Alcoholics Anonymous (1976) *Alcoholics Anonymous* (3rd edn), New York, NY: Alcoholics Anonymous World Services, Inc.

Alcohol Research UK (2010) 'A survey of GPs' knowledge, attitudes and practices on alcohol interventions'. Available at: http:///www.alcoholpolicy.net/2010/02/index.html (accessed 16 May 2012).

Angove, R. and Fothergill, A. (2003) 'Women and alcohol: misrepresented and misunderstood', *Journal of Psychiatric and Mental Health Nursing*, vol 10, no 2, pp 213–19.

Bakhtin, M. (1984 [1965]) *Rabelais and his world* (trans H. Iswolsky), Bloomington, IN: Indiana University Press.

Beresford, P. (2002) 'Thinking about "mental health": towards a social model', *Journal of Mental Health*, vol 11, no 6, pp 581–4.

Blumer, H. (1969) *Social interactionism: perspective and method*, Englewood Cliffs, NJ: Prentice-Hall.

Bowie, F. (2006 [2000]) *The anthropology of religion: an introduction*, Malden, MA: Blackwell Publishing.

Campbell, N.D. (2000) *Using women: gender, drug policy, and social injustice*, New York, NY: Routledge.

Chesler, P. (1997 [1972]) *Women and madness*, New York, NY: Four Walls, Eight Windows.

Coleman, J. S. (1988) 'Social capital in the creation of human capital', *The American Journal of Sociology*, vol 94, Supplement: 'Organizations and Institutions: Sociological and Economic Approaches to the Analysis of Social Structure', pp S95–S120.

Coward, R. (1983) *Patriarchal precedents: sexuality and social relations*, London: Routledge and Kegan Paul.

Cresswell, M. (2009) 'Psychiatric survivors and experiential rights', *Social Policy and Society*, vol 8, no 2, pp 231–43.

Cunningham, J.A. and McCambridge, J. (2012) 'Is alcoholism best viewed as a chronic relapsing disorder?', *Addiction*, vol 107, no 1, pp 6–12.

Deehan, A., Templeton, L., Taylor, C., Drummond, C. and Strang, J. (1998) 'Low detection rates, negative attitudes and the failure to meet the "Health of the Nation" alcohol targets: findings from a national survey of GPs in England and Wales', *Drug and Alcohol Review*, vol 17, no 3, pp 249–58.

Dobash, R.E. and Dobash, R. (1980) *Violence against wives*, London: Open Books.

Eber, C. (2000 [1995]) *Women and alcohol in a highland Maya town: water of hope, water of sorrow*, Austin, TX: University of Texas Press.

Eldridge, A. and Roberts, M. (2008) 'Hen parties: bonding or brawling?', *Drugs: Education, Prevention and Policy*, vol 15, no 3, pp 323–8.

Ettorre, E. (1997) *Women and alcohol: a private pleasure or a public problem?*, London: The Women's Press Ltd.

Ettorre, E. (2007) *Revisioning women and drug use: gender, power and the body*, Basingstoke: Palgrave MacMillan.

Ettorre, E. and Riska, E. (1995) *Gendered moods: psychotropics and society*, London: Routledge.

Fillmore, K.M. (1984) 'When angels fall: women's drinking as cultural preoccupation and as reality', in S.C. Wilsnack and L.J. Beckman (eds) *Alcohol problems in women: The Guilford alcohol studies series*, New York, NY: The Guilford Press.

Goffman, E. (1971 [1959]) *The presentation of self in everyday life*, Harmondsworth: Penguin Books.

Gusfield, J.R. (1996) *Contested meanings: the construction of alcohol problems*, Wisconsin, WI: University of Wisconsin Press.

Hammersley, R. and Reid, M. (2002) 'Why the pervasive addiction myth is still believed', *Addiction Research and Theory*, vol 10, no 1, pp 7–30.

Hausmann, L.R.M., Levine, J.M. and Higgins, E.T. (2008) 'Communication and group perception: extending the '"saying is believing" effect', *Group Processes Intergroup Relations*, vol 11, pp 539–54, DOI: 10.1177/1368430208095405.

Huxley, A. (1932) *Brave new world*, London: Chatto and Windus Ltd.

Itzin, C. (2000) *Home truths about child sexual abuse*, London: Routledge.

Kuhn, T.S. (1970 [1962]) *The structure of scientific revolutions*, Chicago, IL: University of Chicago Press.

Kurtz, E. (1991) *Not-God: a history of Alcoholics Anonymous*, Center City, MN: Hazelden Pittman Archives Press.

Lempp, H. and Seele, C. (2004) 'The hidden curriculum in undergraduate medical education: qualitative study of medical students' perceptions of teaching', *British Medical Journal*, vol 329, pp 770–3.

Lewis, L. (2009) 'Politics of recognition: what can a human rights perspective contribute to understanding users' experiences of involvement in mental health services?', *Social Policy and Society*, vol 6, no 2, pp 257–74.

Lupton, D. (1999) *Risk*, London: Routledge.

Lushin, V. and Anastas, J.W. (2011) 'Harm reduction in substance abuse treatment: pragmatism as an epistemology for social work practice', *Journal of Social Work Practice in the Addictions*, vol 11, no 1, pp 96–100.

McDonald, M. (ed) (1997, 1994) *Gender, drink and drugs: cross-cultural perspectives on women*, vol 10, Oxford: Berg.

Mills, C.W. (2000 [1967]) *The sociological imagination*, Oxford: Oxford University Press.

Moss, H.B., Chen, C.M. and Yi, H.Y. (2007) 'Subtypes of alcohol dependence in a nationally representative sample', *Drug and Alcohol Dependence*, vol 91, nos 2/3, pp 149–58.

Nicholls, J. (2009) *The politics of alcohol: a history of the drink question in England*, Manchester: Manchester University Press.

Oliver, M.J. (1998) 'Theories of disability in health practice and research', *British Medical Journal*, vol 317, no 7170, pp 1446–9.

Penberthy, J.K., Ait-Daoud, N. and Breton, M. (2007) 'Evaluating readiness and treatment seeking effects in a pharmacotherapy trial for alcohol dependence', *Alcoholism: Clinical and Experimental Research*, vol 31, no 9, pp 1538–44.

Perryman, K., Rose, A.K., Winfield, H., Jenner, J., Oyefeso, A., Phillips, T.S., Deluca, P., Heriot-Maitland, C., Galea, S., Cheeta, S., Saunders, V. and Drummond, C. (2011) 'The perceived challenges facing alcohol treatment services in England: a qualitative study of service providers', *Journal of Substance Use*, vol 16, no 1, pp 38–49.

Plant, M.L. (1997) *Women and alcohol: contemporary and historical perspectives*, London: Free Association Books.

Presdee, M. (2000) *Cultural criminology and the carnival of crime*, London: Routledge.

Project MATCH Research Group (1997) 'Matching alcoholism treatments to client heterogeneity: Project MATCH Posttreatment drinking outcomes', *Journal of Studies on Alcohol*, vol 58, no 1, pp 7–29.

Raine, P. (2001) *Women's perspectives on drugs and alcohol: the vicious circle*, Aldershot: Ashgate.

Raistrick, D., Heather, N. and Godfrey, C. (2006) *Review of the effectiveness of treatment for alcohol problems*, London: National Treatment Agency for Substance Misuse.

Reilly, B.M. (2007) 'Viewpoint: "Inconvenient truths about effective clinical teaching"', *The Lancet*, vol 370, no 9588, pp 705–11. Available at: http://linkinghub.elsevier.com/retrieve/pii/S0140673607613476 (accessed 16 May 2012).

Reynaud, M. (2007) 'From the fight against alcoholism to "addictology": shifting the paradigm gives rise to the "Addictions Management Policy" in France', *Editorial: Addiction*, vol 102, no 10, pp 1513–14.

Rose, D. (2001) *Users' voices: the perspective of mental health service users on community and hospital care*, London: The Sainsbury Centre for Mental Health.

Shaw, I. (2004) 'Doctors,"dirty work", patients and "revolving doors"', *Qualitative Health Research*, vol 14, no 8, pp 1032–45.

South, N. (1999) 'Debating drugs and everyday life: mormalisation, prohibition and otherness', in N. South (ed) *Drugs: cultures, controls and everyday life*, London: Sage Publications.

Staddon, P. (2005a) 'Labelling out: the personal account of an ex-alcoholic lesbian feminist', in E. Ettorre (ed) *Making lesbians visible in the substance use field*, New York, NY: The Haworth Press.

Staddon, P. (2005b) 'Making a start', unpublished research report commissioned by Avon and Wiltshire Partners NHS Trust.

Staddon, P. (2009) 'Making whoopee: an exploration of understandings and responses around women's alcohol use', PhD thesis for Department of Sociology, University of Plymouth, UK.

Stein, H.F. (1985) 'Alcoholism as metaphor in American culture: ritual desecration as social integration', *Ethos*, vol 13, no 3, pp 195–235.

Sulkunen, P. (2007) 'Images of addiction: representations of addictions in films', *Addiction Research and Theory*, vol 15, no 6, pp 543–59.

Sweeney, A., Beresford, P., Faulkner, A., Nettle, M. and Rose, D. (2009) *This is survivor research*, Ross On Wye: PCCS Books.

Szasz, T. (1997) *Insanity: the idea and its consequences*, New York, NY: Syracuse University Press.

Thom, B. (1997) 'Women and alcohol: a policy dilemma', *Policy Studies*, vol 18, no 1, pp 49–65.

Traeen, B. and Kvalem, I.L. (1996) 'Sex under the influence of alcohol among Norwegian adolescents', *Addiction*, vol 91, no 7, pp 995–1006.

UKATT (UK alcohol treatment trial) Research Team (2005) 'Effectiveness of treatment for alcohol problems: findings of the randomised UK alcohol treatment trial (UKATT)', *British Medical Journal*, vol 331, no 7516, pp 544–8.

Valentine, G., Holloway, S., Knell, C. and Jayne, M. (2008) 'Drinking places: young people and cultures of alcohol consumption in rural environments', *Journal of Rural Studies*, vol 24, no 1, pp 28–40.

Van Wersch, A. and Walker, W. (2009) 'Binge-drinking in Britain as a social and cultural phenomenon: the development of a grounded theoretical model', *Journal of Health Psychology*, vol 14, no 1, pp 124–34.

Veblen, T. (1994 [1897]) *The theory of the leisure class*, London: Penguin Books.

Velleman, R. and Templeton, L. (2007) 'Understanding and modifying the impact of parents' substance misuse on children', *Advances in Psychiatric Treatment*, vol 13, no 18, pp 79–89.

Wilkinson, R. and Pickett, K. (2009) *The spirit level: why more equal societies almost always do better*, London: Allen Lane.

Willenbring, M.D. (2010) 'The past and future of research on treatment of alcohol dependence', *Alcohol Research and Health, Celebrating 40 Years of Alcohol Research*, vol 33, nos 1/2, pp 55–63.

Wilsnack, S.C. and Beckman, L.J. (ed) (1984) *Alcohol problems in women. The Guilford alcohol studies series*, New York, NY: The Guilford Press.

Winlow, S. (2007) 'T.M. Wilson: *Drinking cultures*. Review', *Sociology* vol 41, no 2, p 373.

Zilberman, M.L., Tavare, H., Blume, S.B. and el-Guebaly, N. (2003) 'Substance use disorders: sex differences and psychiatric co-morbidities', *Canadian Journal of Psychiatry*, vol 8, no 1, pp 5–13.

# NINE

# 'Hard to reach'? Racialised groups and mental health service user involvement

*Jayasree Kalathil*

## Introduction

Engaging people who use mental health services in developing those services, a process generally known as 'user involvement', has developed over the years to become part of policy (DH, 1999, 2005; NIMHE, 2003). Involvement and participation initiatives came on the agenda of most mental health trusts. The National Institute for Mental Health in England (NIMHE) developed a programme and guidelines for user involvement *Making a real difference* (MARD), based on the recommendations from a report on strengthening user and carer involvement in NIMHE (HASCAS, 2005). MARD guidelines and tools for developing and evaluating involvement were expected to enable a systematic approach to user involvement and to fulfil the principles set out in the 2006 White Paper *Our health, our care, our say* (DH, 2006). The National Mental Health Development Unit, which had the responsibility for providing support for the implementation of mental health policy, took this work forward until its closure in March 2011.

The extensive policy changes following the new government in 2010 and the austerity measures that are affecting service delivery across the NHS and social care have made it difficult to be clear about the nature and extent of user involvement in mental health in the future. However, the new mental health strategy, *No health without mental health* (DH, 2011a), contains statements of the Coalition government's commitment to service users, including friends, families and carers, having a say in how services and policy are developed and delivered: 'users of services will increasingly be able to take decisions about their own healthcare. They and their carers may wish to become involved in the planning and design of local services' (DH, 2011a, p 30). Also, the Department of Health is currently funding the National Involvement Partnership, a collaboration between the National Survivor User Network, the Afiya Trust and the Social Perspectives Network. The National Involvement Partnership will develop involvement standards and monitor the impact of user involvement.[1]

User involvement is not just about participating in policy-driven, organisational initiatives. It is also about involving oneself in peer groups, for personal support and/or political campaigning. It is generally seen as enabling and there seems to be a belief in its intrinsic value. That user involvement is central to changing services for the better is based on the idea that service users and survivors are experts in their own experiences and that self-organisation and self-determination are crucial in their journey to recovery. The mental health user movement has long campaigned to bring about this culture shift. However, a closer examination of user involvement in the last few years has shown that people from marginalised and minority groups have not had a substantial role in involvement initiatives (Wallcraft et al, 2003; HASCAS, 2005).

For many service users and survivors from these groups engaged in involvement activities, being 'the only black in the room' in these contexts is a routine experience. While there is a general perception that people from racialised groups[2] and minority backgrounds are 'under-represented' in involvement initiatives, most mainstream efforts to understand this under-representation have started from a point where racialised groups are defined as 'hard to reach'.

In health and social care, the term 'hard to reach' is used to talk about various contexts, including accessing services and care, social marketing, awareness programmes, educational programmes, participation in policy and practice development, and so on. Different communities and people get defined as 'hard to reach' in different contexts. This chapter will examine the formulation and employment of this category against the findings from recent studies based on the experiences of people engaged in user involvement activities in mental health.

## Who is 'hard to reach'?

The term 'hard to reach' is commonly thought to have originated in the context of social marketing (Beder, 1980), where it is thought that there is no one who cannot be reached, it just depends on the approach. However, the usage of the term has become a short cut to refer to disparate populations and communities who pose difficulties to conventional ways of doing things. For example, the Health and

Safety Executive defines 'hard to reach' as those communities or groups that are 'inaccessible to most traditional and conventional methods' (Whitnell, 2004, p 8) and their list of identified 'hard to reach' groups includes 'self-employed farmers' (an almost specific category) and 'ethnic minorities' (a highly problematic generalisation).

Certain communities or groups may not engage with a specific programme or service for a range of reasons. The problem with using a term like 'hard to reach' to define these groups is that it assumes homogeneity within disparate groups and places the problem within the group rather than the approaches used to enable engagement (Brackertz, 2007). The communities that are routinely grouped under the term have been called obstinate, disadvantaged, illiterate, information-poor and chronically uninformed (Freimuth and Mettger, 1990). In mental health service user involvement, racialised groups seen as 'hard to reach' have been defined as difficult and separatist (Kalathil, 2009). The onus for participation and involvement is placed on the communities identified as 'hard to reach': they are the problem and not the ways in which involvement is defined or undertaken. An important first step in changing this status quo is to understand the reasons for the perceived under-representation of mental health service users from racialised groups in user involvement initiatives.

## Issues in user involvement

How is it that a diverse range of racialised groups, all captured under the term 'black and minority ethnic (BME) communities', all with different histories of engagement with mental health services, self-help, community development and direct experience, have been placed within this category called 'hard to reach'? Nasa Begum (2006) identified several myths surrounding marginalised communities and their participation, many of which are used to justify the 'hard to reach' label: 'We don't know what they want'; 'They are not interested in participating'; 'We work with community leaders and the black voluntary sector'; and 'The service user movement represents everybody'.

These justifications have been analysed by several recent studies on the participation of service users from racialised groups in user involvement initiatives (Blakey, 2005; Begum, 2006; Kalathil, 2009). Several key themes emerge. First, there seems to be a view that the mainstream definition of user involvement – specific activities involving service users, often driven by policy and defined by the organisation setting up these initiatives – did not acknowledge the work that many people were doing within their communities to bring about an understanding of mental health and attitudes towards it. In this sense, rather than thinking about the under-representation of people from racialised groups in mainstream initiatives, we need to start thinking about nurturing and supporting work that is already happening within local communities (Kalathil, 2009).

Second, research over the years has shown that people from racialised groups continue to experience compulsory, coercive and unequal treatment within mental health services. For example, evidence shows that:

- while there has been a fall in the overall number of inpatients in mental health services, the number of people detained in hospitals has risen, for a third consecutive time, for people from some racialised groups, with proportions of people from black or black British groups rising from 53.9% in 2008/09 to 66.3% in 2009/10 (NHS Information Centre, 2011);
- rates of admission, detention and seclusion continue to be higher than average for people from racialised groups (CQC, 2011); and
- a larger proportion of people from some minority ethnic communities, than might be expected from the detained population, are liable to be issued a community treatment order (CTO) (Lawton-Smith, 2010); rates for being placed on a CTO were higher among the South Asian and black groups by 22%–106% (CQC, 2011).

Given the high levels of coercion and compulsion in their experience of mental health services, many people may feel the need to leave damaging experiences behind. Those who do want to continue engaging with developing services find that user involvement spaces rarely provide the space for discussing and resolving the effects of these negative experiences (Blakey, 2006; Kalathil, 2009). They tend to assume that service users/survivors and services can start working together without addressing the discriminatory practices that continue to influence the way in which services are delivered. To quote a participant in the *Dancing to our own tunes* consultation:

> The stark reality is that for a lot of people, particularly young people from minority groups, their experience of involvement is around the harsh end of services. So they are thinking, what's that got to do with me? How is [user involvement] going to change the way I'm going to be sectioned and carted off from my house to the ward? They

don't see the connection between me being involved in influencing policy on the one side when I'm out and how that's going to impact on the way I'm treated when I'm in hospital or even in the community for that matter. (Kalathil, 2009, p 24)

Blakey (2006) notes that the Department of Health, in its statement about patient and public involvement, posits an ideal situation, where participants of these forums may rarely need to be adversarial, and will be positive and collaborative. But, she argues, unless these spaces explored the emotional journeys, the negative and difficult experiences that people have been through, it is less likely that people will feel able to engage. The disempowerment people experience within services reinforces the scepticism that a lot of people have about the meaning and usefulness of user involvement.

Involvement spaces can also be disempowering spaces by reflecting the kind of racial bias and overt racism that exist in society. Experiences of encountering racism in various contexts of involvement – within service-led initiatives (like trust committees), within user/peer groups and within the mainstream mental health movement – have been explored in some studies (Trivedi, 2008; Kalathil, 2009). Being a token 'black' person in an initiative whose structures and parameters are set up in a way that intimidates and silences one's cultural and/or racial identities is a common experience for many people. In user-led spaces, the focus was on user/survivor identities and there was pressure to separate this part of your identity from other markers of identity, such as that of 'race', community or culture, or experiences of racialisation (Kalathil, 2009, pp 14–15). Racist attitudes in all these spaces worked to silence and intimidate those who were faced with it, until they ultimately withdrew. The user movement, it was felt, had learned to fight against the discrimination faced by people with psychiatric diagnoses, but it had not been successful in extending that learning to speak up when people were discriminated against because of their race or ethnicity.

One of the main criticisms about user involvement in general has been that it has not given any real decision-making powers to service users. Hodge (2005) has shown how power is used discursively in user involvement initiatives in apparently trivial ways to ensure that the normative hierarchies of institutional spaces and practices are protected. Carr (2004, p 14) reminds us that the idea of 'care' and the history of service provision in a welfare state are rooted in a hierarchy of power:

The traditional division between service user and professional is rooted in the history of 'welfare' in the UK. Historically, people who use social services were seen as passive recipients of charity and care. Decision-making power about that care traditionally lay in the hands of the providers, as did the opportunity to assert expertise.

This hierarchy of power is replicated in user involvement spaces and initiatives when professionals continue to hold on to the role of the expert and authority, agendas are pre-set and decisions already made, and merely having some service users around the table is seen as equality enough. Participating as a token representative in these situations can aggravate feelings of disempowerment already felt as a result of discriminatory experiences based on one's racial identity, mental health status and position in society. For service users from racialised groups, power imbalances in these settings arise not only from that of the professional–patient hierarchy, but also from experiences of marginalisation and discrimination based on 'race', ethnicity and culture (Trivedi, 2008).

Many user-led mainstream initiatives, research projects and campaigns also perpetuated these power hierarchies. In user-led research, for example, users and survivors from minority communities are often approached only as research subjects or participants, while they are not given any part in designing, developing or carrying out the research, pointing to the continuing existence of a 'hierarchy of credibility' (Becker, 1967). Participating in involvement initiatives with no real power was often experienced as furthering the disempowerment that service users/survivors from racialised groups already faced on account of their racial identity, mental distress and position in society. Some participants had made a conscious decision not to be involved in these initiatives unless there was a clear indication that the organisation was committed to changing the hierarchies and that they had influence over decision-making. Tew (2005) suggests that some service users may be trying to regain some power by making a conscious decision not to get involved, a suggestion borne out by the findings of other consultations (Kalathil, 2009).

In the context of all the experiences just described, it was clear that involvement in mainstream initiatives as token members of minority communities had lost its appeal. The need now, for many people, was to work on agendas and issues that were specific to the communities and contexts that they were working with. It was important to understand the purpose of involvement, how much influence a person has in the process and how much capacity and will there is within the organisation to bring about change before engaging in involvement activities.

## Delivering race equality: the Ambassadors programme

Perhaps the only consolidated national programme for user/carer involvement aimed at people from racialised groups so far was offered by the Delivering Race Equality (DRE) Ambassadors programme. The programme ran from 2007 to 2010 (in the early months as the Champions programme).

The DRE programme (DH, 2005) was launched after the inquiry into the death of David Bennett (NSCSHA, 2003) forcefully highlighted the need to tackle racial inequality in mental health service delivery. The Ambassadors programme aimed to link communities into the overall DRE programme and strategic developments so that they could influence and improve the outcomes and experiences of mental health services for racialised groups. The structure to do this was a national network of independent service users/survivors and carers who would represent the voices and views of their local/regional communities.

The programme was successful in bringing together dedicated and creative people. However, whether the ambassadors had any influence over the DRE programme and its agenda as a whole is doubtful. An evaluation of the programme undertaken by the Social Perspectives Network showed that 'wider application and roll-out of the work was limited and there were structures and systems that acted as a barrier to the successful and effective implementation of the programme' (Bogg, 2011, p 5). The evaluation highlighted these key problems:

- insufficient and changing structures and processes affecting stability and consolidation of involvement;
- lack of role in decision-making affecting the ambassadors' influence over the race equality agenda and its national, regional and local delivery;
- inconsistent application of the ambassador model and support for it across the country;
- questions about the representativeness of ambassadors; and
- lack of clarity of purpose and about demonstrating outcomes – ambassadors as 'add-on' to the existing programme.

A key question to ask is why a government-led national involvement programme was set up by hand-picking individuals, while local, regional and national user-led groups and networks of black and minority ethnic service users and carers already existed. National programmes for black and minority ethnic service user involvement would have had more credibility, influence and, arguably, a lasting legacy if they had supported and sustained already-existing alliances of service users working together, sharing learning and supporting each other. Instead, the service users were expected to be ambassadors for a programme whose parameters had already been set up, rather than being involved at a stage when those parameters were being set up and being ambassadors for the communities and regions they represent.

## Not that hard to reach: redefining user involvement

It is clear that there are several factors that need to change within mainstream user involvement initiatives. However, a more fundamental task is to redefine user involvement itself. The mainstream definition of service user involvement excluded a lot of the work that people were doing on the ground, within their communities. The idea of 'increasing involvement of hard-to-reach communities' seemed to propose the need to ensure more 'black bodies' on committees, beneficiary numbers and research subjects, without examining organisational cultures that viewed marginalised communities as 'hard to reach'. If service users and survivors from racialised groups are to participate meaningfully in user involvement initiatives, there has to be 'structural changes in hierarchies, ways of working, assumptions, power structures within institutions, resource allocation, the location of decision making and the way people are treated within mental health systems and outside them' (Kalathil, 2009, p 12). In order to do this, we need to ask some key questions before setting up user involvement initiatives:

- Is the service/organisation setting up the user involvement initiative convinced that the involvement of service users from racialised groups is necessary for service development? Or is it soliciting their involvement to tick equality assessment boxes?
- Has the initiative set out supportive and safe spaces for discussing people's experiences and emotional journeys if appropriate and necessary?
- Is there a willingness to examine organisational (including clinical) practices and hierarchies?
- What is the service users' role – advising, taking decisions, designing services, consultative? Is there clarity about how their contributions will be made use of?

- Are structures in place to value people's contributions, both through recognition of their expertise and by paying them adequately?
- In non-statutory/user-led groups, does the group provide supportive spaces for the articulation of all identities and the incorporation of them into work priorities and practices?

## Implications for current practice

The real reason for the underutilisation of the potential and expertise of service users from racialised groups, we have seen, is the existence of policies and practices that make it hard for mainstream organisations to reach out to communities. In a context where much of the existing policies and procedures have changed, how will user involvement feature as an important mechanism for developing and delivering equitable mental health services and how much say will service users from racialised groups have in this?

As stated at the beginning of this chapter, the importance of user involvement in continuing to develop and deliver equitable mental health services, it would seem, is supported by the new mental health strategy and in policies affecting health and social care delivery in general. The new mechanism to involve the public, including service users and their families and carers, in influencing mental health services is the Local HealthWatch, introduced in the NHS White Paper, *Equity and excellence: liberating the NHS* (DH, 2011b). Local HealthWatch is expected to feed into the new 'consumer champion', HealthWatch England, based within the Care Quality Commission, and through it into the National Commissioning Board. The role of HealthWatch England in the context of mental health, according to the mental health strategy, is:

> to ensure that the voices of people with mental health problems, including children, young people and their families – who can often be marginalised – are central to the assessment of quality in specialist mental health services and in health services more generally. (DH, 2011a, p 53)

However, the mental health strategy document does not contain a clear implementation plan to show how marginalised groups of people who will already be on the lower rungs of local social hierarchies will be supported to participate in Local HealthWatch and make decisions for themselves. There is concern that involvement structures such as HealthWatch are shifting the focus away from mental health and towards the generic engagement of 'patients'. The 'parity of esteem' between mental health and physical health, celebrated in the new mental health strategy call to action, while theoretically moving mental health away from its stigmatised position, may have a detrimental effect on what say mental health service users have in how the NHS is run and how services are commissioned (Kalathil, 2011).

This is compounded for racialised groups. The 'call to action' on the mental health strategy has been criticised for not including any user-led organisations or organisations working with racialised groups (The Afiya Trust, 2011). The closure of the DRE programme, while failing to address institutional racism, and the continuing racial inequalities within mental health services have made several services users, communities and campaigners feel that race equality is taking a back seat in mental health policy. The perceived 'disappearance' of the race equality agenda from mental health policy is also linked to the shift to a 'single equalities' mode of working. Towards the end of the DRE programme, and in keeping with the Equality Act 2010, there was a clear steer in policy towards a broader equalities agenda, and this is carried through in the new mental health strategy. While there are benefits in working across equality issues, this should not be at the expense of neglecting key issues for communities.

For example, it has been pointed out that unless specific issues affecting groups of people are addressed strategically, it would be entirely possible to achieve the six shared objectives of the new mental health strategy overall while leaving behind sections of society already experiencing disproportionate, inappropriate and discriminatory treatment within mental health services. Crepaz-Keay (2011, p 19), for example, argues that whether you achieve the six objectives in the strategy will depend on:

> where you live, what you earn, how old you are, what your diagnosis is, whether you have any other disabilities, what colour your skin is. This matters because it is entirely possible to achieve all six objectives without making a jot of difference to a single young black man with schizophrenia. Will this be different in five years' time?

There have also been substantial cuts to public funding and resources for community and voluntary-sector organisations, crucially affecting their role in supporting and sustaining user involvement activities and opportunities. While the impact of cuts on organisations working specifically with the mental health of racialised groups is yet to emerge coherently, the broader impact on this sector is already established. One study shows that 45% of all BME voluntary-sector groups had faced funding cuts from local authorities, in addition to 61% who faced cuts in government funding, other grant-making trusts and the Big Lottery, even as 77% of the sector had experienced a sharp rise in requests for services as people feel increasingly vulnerable (CEMVO, 2010).

A recent review carried out by the National Survivor User Network of the work done following the publication of the 2009 report *Dancing to our own tunes* (Kalathil, 2011) showed that there was an increased acknowledgement of the fact that it was unacceptable to continue categorising communities and groups as 'hard to reach' in public participation and user involvement. However, the political will and the policy context ensuring the involvement of mental health service users from racialised groups were weaker and the resources and structures to sustain them were diminishing, despite the increasing visibility and strength of user-led groups generally, and those from racialised backgrounds in particular.

In this context, partnership-working across all user/survivor groups and between user-led and non-user-led groups is even more important in continuing to challenge racism and discrimination in user spaces within and outside mental health services and in influencing decisions about mental health care. No communities are, by definition, 'hard to reach'. However, as we have seen, there are practices, prejudices, belief systems and experiences that collude to create the exclusion of some communities from involvement initiatives, whether they are mental health services-led, voluntary sector-led or as part of the larger mental health movement. Unless these are examined and dismantled, many people will echo the sentiment of one of the participants in the *Dancing to our own tunes* consultation: 'sometimes you just have to walk away and say you're not interested' (Kalathil, 2009, p 26).

## Notes

[1] For more information, see www.nsun.org.uk

[2] The term 'racialised groups' is used to refer to groups and communities who are subjected to a range of social, cultural, institutional and psychological 'racialisation' processes by which they are made inferior and seen as different and deficient because of their 'race', ethnicity, skin colour, national origins, religion and so on. For the uses, abuses, problems and possibilities of this formulation, see Murji and Solomos (2005).

## References

Becker, H.S. (1967) 'Whose side are we on', *Social Problems*, vol 14, pp 240–7.

Beder, H.W. (1980) 'Reaching the hard-to-reach adult through effective marketing', *New Directions for Continuing Education*, no 8, pp 11–26.

Begum, N. (2006) *Doing it for themselves: participation and black and minority ethnic service users*, London: SCIE/REU.

Blakey, H. (2005) *Participation, why bother? The views of black and minority ethnic mental health service users on participation in the NHS in Bradford*, Bradford: International Centre for Participation Studies.

Blakey, H. (2006) 'Participation: why bother?', *Mental Health Today*, May, pp 23–6.

Bogg, D. (2011) *DRE ambassadors evaluation report*, London: National Mental Health Development Unit.

Brackertz, N. (2007) 'Who is hard to reach and why?', ISR working paper, The Swinburne Institute of Social Research, Victoria.

Carr, S. (2004) *Has service user participation made a difference to social care services?*, London: Social Care Institute of Excellence.

CEMVO (Council of Ethnic Minority Voluntary Sector Organisations) (2010) *Report on the impact of economic downturn on black and minority ethnic third sector organisations*, London: Council for Ethnic Minority Voluntary Organisations.

CQC (Care Quality Commission) (2011) *Results of the 2010 national census of inpatients and patients on supervised community treatment in mental health and learning disability services in England and Wales*, London: CQC.

Crepaz-Keay, D. (2011) 'Measuring success of objectives', *Open Mind*, no 165, p 19.

DH (Department of Health) (1999) *National service framework for mental health: modern standards and service models*, London: Department of Health.

DH (2005) *Delivering race equality in mental health care: an action plan for reform inside and outside services*, London: Department of Health.

DH (2006) *Our health, our care, our say: a new direction for community services*, London: Department of Health.

DH (2011a) *No health without mental health: a cross-government mental health outcomes strategy for people of all ages*, London: Department of Health.

DH (2011b) *Equity and excellence: liberating the NHS*, London: Department of Health.

Freimuth, V.S. and Mettger, W. (1990) 'Is there a hard-to-reach audience?', *Public Health Reports*, vol 105, no 3, pp 232–8.

HASCAS (Health and Social Care Advisory Service) (2005) *Making a real difference: strengthening service user and carer involvement in NIMHE*, London: NIMHE.

Hodge, S (2005) 'Participation, discourse and power: a case study in service user involvement', *Critical Social Policy*, vol 25, no 2, pp 164–79.

Kalathil, J. (2009) *Dancing to our own tunes: reassessing black and minority ethnic mental health service user involvement*, London: NSUN.

Kalathil, J. (2011) *Dancing to our own tunes: reprint of the 2008 report with a review of work undertaken to take the recommendations forward*, London: NSUN.

Murji, K. and Solomos, J. (2005) *Racialization: studies in theory and practice*, Oxford: Oxford University Press.

NHS Information Centre (2011) *Mental health bulletin: fourth report from mental health minimum dataset (MHMDS) annual returns 2010*, Leeds: HSC Information Centre.

NIMHE (National Institute for Mental Health in England) (2003) *Engaging and changing: developing effective policy for the care and treatment of black and minority ethnic detained patients*, London: National Institute for Mental Health in England.

NSCSHA (Norfolk, Suffolk and Cambridgeshire Strategic Health Authority) (2003) *Independent inquiry into the death of David Bennett*, Cambridge: Norfolk, Suffolk and Cambridgeshire Strategic Health Authority.

Tew, J. (2005) 'Power relations, social order and mental health', in J. Tew (ed) *Social perspectives in mental health*, London: Jessica Kingsley.

The Afiya Trust (2011) '"Disparity of esteem" for BME communities in new mental health strategy leads to call for action on race equality', Press release, 11 February.

Trivedi, P. (2008) 'Black service user involvement: rhetoric or reality?', in S. Fernando and F. Keating (eds) *Mental health in a multi-ethnic society*, London: Routledge.

Wallcraft, J., Read, J. and Sweeney, A. (2003) *On our own terms: users and survivors of mental health services working together for support and change*, London: The Sainsbury Centre for Mental Health.

Whitnell, S. (2004) *Successful interventions with hard to reach groups*, Basingstoke: Health and Safety Executive.

# TEN

# Individual narratives and collective knowledge: capturing lesbian, gay and bisexual service user experiences

*Sarah Carr*

Behind the story I tell is the one I don't. Behind the story you hear is the one I wish I could make you hear. (Allison, 1996, p 39)

Even in my earliest storytelling I saw myself as overcoming adverse situations. (Hammer, 2010, p 9)

## Introduction

This chapter explores the idea of capturing individual testimony to contribute to collective knowledge on lesbian, gay and bisexual (LGB) experiences of mental distress and mental health service use. The exploration draws upon some of my own reflections about the methodologies I have used in some of my own research, where I use personal experience both as a starting point and as a form of inquiry and then locate individual accounts as part of collective user and survivor knowledge. I attempt to situate this within the wider tradition of the use of experiential knowledge, narrative and testimony in user and survivor research. I also link the use of personal narrative to the development of individual and collective identity for LGB people. Finally, I examine the potential of autoethnography to provide a viable methodology for capturing personal testimony, experience and narrative for research on mental health and LGB people.

## Marginalised memoirs and collective knowledge

Beginning with some brief contextualisation, personal narrative and first-hand experiential accounts of mental distress have not historically been valued as knowledge equal to that of professionally trained clinicians and practitioners (Beresford, 2000, 2003; Turner and Beresford, 2005; Tew et al, 2006; Sweeney et al, 2009). However, it is useful to note that one of the only encounters Sigmund Freud had with a person who experienced what would now be termed 'psychotic symptoms' was through the detailed memoirs of a man who had been diagnosed with 'dementia praecox' – now known as schizophrenia. Published in 1903, Daniel Schreber's *Memoirs of my nervous illness* (Schreber, 2000) gave a unique insight into his thoughts, beliefs and experiences and could arguably count as one of the first pieces of user research into mental distress. Schreber himself was the subject of his own investigation and the result was a personal account of his experience of 'psychosis'. Freud then went on to psychoanalyse Schreber's memoirs in an attempt to establish a psychoanalytic understanding of psychosis (Freud, 2002). Much later, a groundbreaking user-led research project brought together the individual testimonies of people who had been subjected to Electro-Convulsive Therapy (ECT). Collectively, these personal narratives about memory loss as a side-effect formed a body of knowledge with which to challenge the prevailing clinical research evidence on information, consent and the side effects of ECT, and were eventually accepted as valid evidence (Rose et al, 2005). Instead of people whose lives had been affected by ECT being represented by clinicians with no first-hand knowledge of the treatment effects, the user-researchers focused on bringing together a wider representative body of knowledge based on experience and testimony to further understanding of this intervention, its side effects and informed consent.

Historically, LGB lives and ways of managing mental distress have been characterised by others as invisible, marginal, dangerous and deviant (Carr, 2011a). Even recent research on LGB service users and carers in mental health and social care, particularly older people, resurfaces the concept of 'invisibility' (Fish, 2009; Fenge and Hicks, 2011). This concept of 'invisibility' reflects the fact that we have seldom been respectfully represented by others and have even more rarely been able to truthfully represent ourselves. However, over the past 50 years, LGB people in the US and UK have gradually 'come out' and established a tradition of self-representation, often drawing on autobiography, experience and history, in cinema and literature. The lesbian film-maker and artist Barbara Hammer, credited with creating the first 'lesbian-made' film about lesbians in 1974, highlighted the theme of visibility in her 'Invisible Histories' film trilogy (Hammer and Taylor, 2007). Authors like Jeanette Winterson and Audre Lorde have drawn explicitly on autobiographical accounts of growing up gay (Lorde, 2001; Winterson, 2001) and the sociologist Elizabeth Ettorre is credited with being one of the first lesbians to produce a sociological account of lesbian lives (Ettorre, 1980). Interestingly, Ettorre has also explored the use of autoethnography in sociology (Ettorre, 2010). Such direct, personal accounts and narrative artefacts have made huge contributions to the way LGB people understand ourselves personally and politically as individuals and as communities (Plummer, 1995). They also form a type of 'coming out', which can involve the use of self and personal narrative as counter-evidence in political, civil and human rights campaigning (Blasius, 1994). As Heaphy notes: 'recent theories highlight the creative agency involved in responding to social and legal marginalisation' (Heaphy, 2009, p 121). However, despite the considerable body of autobiographical work by LGB people, explicit, specific accounts by LGB people with mental health problems about their lives and experiences remain relatively rare, particularly in research. A notable exception is a 2004 study by Smith, Bartlett and King entitled 'Treatments of homosexuality in Britain since the 1950s – an oral history: the experience of patients' (Smith et al, 2004), where the authors collected the personal stories of 29 LGB people who had undergone aversion therapy and other types of interventions to attempt to alter their sexuality in the NHS psychiatric system. The research was a pioneering effort to understand the effects of psychiatric treatment on LGB people as it analysed the aggregated personal testimonies of a group of people who had been 'patients'. Despite this important contribution to knowledge, stories of how LGB people have coped with mental distress, pathologisation and discrimination in mental health services remain rare and the work I discuss here is an effort to contribute to the collective knowledge about LGB mental health and service use.

## Reflections on my use of personal narrative in research

In this section, I present an examination of how I have conducted my own inquiries into my personal experience as a gay woman who has experienced varying degrees of mental distress (including using self-harm as a way to manage it) and used a wide range of mental health services for over 20 years (from primary care and long-term psychotherapy to locked ward and poly-pharmacy). My personal narrative includes what Cronin et al call 'the caring encounter', in my case, encounters with formal mental health services, which then 'constitutes part of a life-*story*, constructed by the individuals themselves' (Cronin et al, 2011, p 426). The reflections here are drawn from a chapter of my PhD, where I explored and accounted for the methodological approaches I used for particular investigations into LGB mental distress and service use. The particular works to which I refer are Carr's (2005, 2011a, 2011b).

These articles contain autobiographical material, personal narrative or accounts of lived experience. Carr (2005) has been recognised as an example of the use of 'auto-ethnography, reflexive and personal narrative methodologies' for 'researching, learning and writing about lesbian and gay issues' (Trotter et al, 2006, p 373), and has the potential to contribute to the emerging body of 'queer methodologies' (Browne and Nash, 2010). Because of the 'lived experience' dimension, the works could come within the broad category of 'mental health user/survivor research', such as Sweeney et al (2009), Rose (2004) and Beresford and Wallcraft (1997), albeit one that does not involve the production of primary research studies, but, rather, attempts to undertake a 'storytelling research process', which Wilkins (2000, p 147) describes as: 'the recasting of personal stories in the light of ... pre-existing stories (which may include anecdotes or the literature) and the production of an encapsulating account'.

Part of the endeavour is to begin to make 'collective sense of individual stories' (Wilkins, 2000, p 147), in this case, my own stories and those I gather from the literature, thereby combining research review methodology with reflections on personal experience, and partially addressing the problem of 'personal experience versus the scientific method' in some emancipatory research (Humphries, 2000). To refer to the reflexivity theories of Alvesson and Skoldberg, they advocate maintaining a personal awareness of perspective and interpretation rather than polarising into opposing methodological approaches that seek to establish 'truths'. Further, they note how maintaining reflexivity in the research process means that:

> serious attention is paid to the way different kinds of linguistic, social, political and theoretical elements are woven together in the process of knowledge development, during which empirical material is constructed, interpreted and written ... this ... can provide an important basis for a generation of knowledge that opens up rather than closes, and furnishes opportunities for understanding, rather than establishes truths. (Alvesson and Skoldberg, 2009, p 9)

Although Barnes has been critical of the use of biographical accounts in emancipatory disability research, citing the risk of sentimentality, medicalisation and potential for only weak political impact (Barnes, 2003), establishing new perspectives through the use of individual narrative has been highlighted as having a potential contribution to make to evidence-based practice in mental health (Greenhalgh and Hurwitz, 1998; Roberts, 2000), because 'the subjective, personal, patient story and the interpretative, scientific, medical story are not translations of each other but independently co-existing narratives' (Hunter, 1991, cited in Roberts, 2000, p 434). Further to this, Roberts describes the importance of narrative processes for understanding mental distress, and his observation about the effect of 'toxic stories' on mental health is particularly relevant to these works, in the context of their emancipatory intention (Barnes, 1992; Oliver, 1996):

> Some grow up with life-denying meanings and are hostage to toxic stories that adversely define and constrain their identity and self-image. They are caught in a story, and the task is first to understand this and then to find ways of modifying (re-authoring) these myths-people-live-by to promote a more constructive, effective and adaptive context for living. (Roberts, 2000, p 435)

For these three works, my particular standpoint (Harding, 1993) and methods of knowledge production can be partly explained with reference to the work of Frye (1983), as described in Stanley (1990, p 33): 'a lesbian feminist epistemology ... brought into existence out of an explicit consciousness of oppression, out of silences, intrusions, misnamings'. Here, I am also guided by emancipatory research principles, defined by disability activist researchers as 'openness, participation, accountability' (Barnes, 1992, p 121) and 'empowerment and reciprocity' (Oliver, 1996, p 30). Moreover, as Stone and Priestley (1996, p 706) have asserted, it is important that emancipatory research has 'the ability to give voice to the personal [and] to legitimise previously marginalised voices', while others emphasise the importance of reflexivity: the way that disabled people may be empowered within the processes of emancipatory research (Barnes, 2003). Therefore, these works are emancipatory in their endeavour and are guided by the appropriate principles, particularly the 'social model of madness and distress', as defined by mental health service users and survivors (Beresford and Wallcraft, 1997). Broadly, the topics and investigations of the three articles fit with the research investigations suggested by survivor researchers as being important for further understanding this 'social model of madness and distress' (Beresford et al, 2010) and social perspectives on mental health:

> Social causes of madness and distress; medicalisation of our experience and distress; the destructive and discriminatory response from both psychiatry and broader society; the need for a social response to the distress and disablement which survivors experience, addressing the social origins and relations of their distress, instead of being restricted to people's individual difficulties. (Beresford and Wallcraft, 1997, p 83)

However, to return to the use of self, autobiography and personal narrative, it needs to be noted that the majority of thinking about the use of reflexivity and biography in the research process concerns addressing the relationship between the researcher and the researched (Chamberlayne et al, 2000; Finlay and Gough, 2003; Alvesson and Skoldberg, 2009; Merril and West, 2009). Self-disclosure and self-awareness in the social research process are ways of addressing the need for other-awareness of the research 'subjects' (Shakespeare et al, 1993). Similarly, the model of feminist 'praxis' and 'auto/biography' focuses on researcher–subject relations (Stanley, 1990, 1993). However, these three works review existing literature (in which I appear as the research subject or conceptual 'problem' [ie the gay person or the mad person or both]) through the application of experiential knowledge and personal biography in order to reposition knowledge, reframe the 'self' (which includes experience and behaviour), add to the collective knowledge of a marginalised group (LGB people with mental health problems) and offer a new perspective that others who identify with my story can use for their own empowerment. Despite this, the principles and methodology of reflexivity and autobiography are also relevant for this endeavour. In some cases, I am interpreting and understanding my own experience through research and policy analysis to construct counter-knowledge from the margins (see hooks, 1990a): 'The auto/biographical "I" is an inquiring analytic sociological agent who is concerned in constructing rather than "discovering" social reality and social knowledge' (Stanley, 1993, p 49).

Humphries (2000, p 188) has warned that, 'as researchers, commitment to self-reflexivity is fundamental, although this can deteriorate into self-indulgence which places the researcher as the norm'. Alvesson and Skoldberg argue that a reflexive methodological approach is important so that 'confessionalism' does not slip into 'self-absorption' and 'self-reflective isolationism': 'reflexivity, in the research context means paying attention to these aspects without letting any one of them dominate. In other words, it is a question of avoiding empiricism, narcissism and different varieties of social and linguistic reductionism' (Alvesson and Skoldberg, 2009, p 269). It could be that some of my research could be dismissed as 'self-indulgent' by some readers, but part of my intention in self-disclosure is to make visible what has been invisible in research and policy – that is, the personal stories and direct, unmediated experiences of people with mental health problems and/or LGB people *in our own voice*. Where possible, I position my experience within a historical continuum (especially the history of psychiatry) and alongside that of others but do not claim that my personal narrative is representative or universal. Rather, I suggest that some of my experiences may be shared by others and can contribute to collective service user knowledge (Beresford, 2003). Thereby, I aim to offer an example of my own life account produced by myself that challenges the accounts about me or 'my kind' as determined by others, as Goodley and Clough (2004, p 336) have argued for research conducted in the context of post-modernity: 'expert discourses are being challenged by exposing their narrative construction ... [and] grand political and cultural narratives are under attack by personalised and localised narratives'. My exploratory works have been produced in response to my own critical question as a research *subject* about 'Who benefits from the research?' (Truman, 2000). In my position as the '*other*', the works are produced from what bell hooks describes as 'marginality as site of resistance' (hooks, 1990a), one in which I reclaim the position of 'author and authority' (hooks, 1990b). Perhaps bell hooks provides the best account of the conditions in which most of these three articles were produced and why they were produced:

> I am waiting for them to stop talking about the 'other', to stop even describing how important it is to be able to speak about difference.... Often this speech about the 'other' is also a mast, an oppressive talk hiding gaps, absences, that space where our words would be if we were speaking, if there was a silence, if we were there.... This 'we' is that 'us' in the margins, that 'we' who inhabit marginal space that is not a site of domination, but a place of resistance.... Often this speech about the 'other' annihilates, erases: 'no need to hear your voice when I can talk about you better than you can speak about yourself. No need to hear your voice ...

> I want to know your story. And then I will tell it back to
> you in a new way ... I am still author, authority'. (hooks,
> 1990b, pp 151–2)

For example, in my personal exploration of self-harm, '"A chance to
cut is a chance to cure": self harm and self protection' (Carr, 2011a),
I attempt to use my marginalisation as a site of resistance, as hooks
suggests. Essentially, I would argue that this work is told by a silenced
voice but in a way that uses 'an encapsulating account' of personal
narrative and research to challenge and resist dominant and oppressive
perspectives on self-harm and sexuality in the psychiatric system. I
write that:

> I acknowledge my perspective is a unique one and I do not
> claim to speak for all those touched by the same experiences
> as me, but I hope this chapter will act as a voice crying out
> from the data. (Carr, 2011a, p 32)

This work featured strongly in my later thinking about the potential
of autoethnography for LGB user and survivor research, as it could
provide a framework for silenced voices and untold stories, like those
of a gay self-harmer, to be told.

## Voice and visibility: the potential of autoethnography

In this section, I briefly outline some of the key ideas about
autoethnography and examine how this methodology could have
the potential to transfer to user and survivor research, particularly for
LGB people. As noted earlier, a work in which I discuss some of my
own experiences in the mental health system (Carr, 2005) has been
cited in the literature as an example of 'autoethnography' (Trotter et al,
2006), despite the fact that I did not intentionally use the methodology
and was, indeed, later prompted to research its relevance following
the association with my work. In addition, I had not come across the
explicit use of the methodology in user and survivor research before.
So, this section is an attempt to sketch out what autoethnography could
contribute to mental health research that uses testimony, experiential
knowledge and autobiographical material, such as personal narrative,
particularly for LGB people.

Over the past 20 years, autoethnography has developed as a
sociological methodology to address some of the challenges about
traditional research claims to objectivity, authority and universality,

which have their parallels in mental health and social care (Ellis and Bochner, 2000; Witkin, 2000). For example, the type of critique about traditional ethnographers 'authoritatively entering a culture, exploiting cultural members and then recklessly leaving to write about the culture for … professional gain' (Ellis et al, 2011, p 2) has distinct similarities to the criticisms of disability research by founders of emancipatory research (Barnes, 1992; Oliver, 1996). Very briefly described, 'autoethnography is an approach to research and writing that seeks to describe and systematically analyse personal experience in order to understand cultural experience' (Ellis et al, 2011, p 1). Further, it has been argued that 'autoethnographic texts create the possibility for a reclamation of voices that have been either absent from traditional social science texts or have been misrepresented as ways to understand whole schemas of cultures' (Tierney, 1998, p 66). The idea of autoethnography came from considering what it could mean for the social sciences if *stories* rather than *theories* were proffered, and if research became explicitly value-centred, rather than claiming to be value-free (Bochner, 1994). While the methodology is debated and contested (Tierney, 1998; Anderson, 2006; Muncey, 2006; Tolich, 2010), it has been used: to inform research with disabled people (Petersen, 2011); as a way for people with mental health problems to explore the nature of stigma and marginalisation (Muncey and Robinson, 2007); as a means of 'sensemaking' to analyse personally traumatic experiences, such as bullying (Vickers, 2007); to capture sensory, non-clinical knowledge by those who have experienced being in intensive care (Uotinen, 2011); and to capture other 'illness narratives' (Richards, 2008). Interestingly, in the US, autoethnography has also been applied in training for mental health practitioners, with one notable account detailing a woman's struggle to understand and overcome her own homophobia (McLaurin, 2003).

There are some themes emerging from the developing work on autoethnographic methodology that seem particularly relevant for user and survivor research generally, and for that conducted by LGB people in particular. Richards, who uses autoethnography to document the experience of kidney failure, transplantation and recovery, argues that this is often 'written about by outsiders (medical practitioners, care providers, academics), whereas the insider's (patient's) expertise is occluded' (Richards, 2008, p 1717). Here, she positions the centrality of the 'insider voice' and surfaces the theme of invisibility, both of which are reflected in user and survivor research by LGB people as well as more generally in user and survivor research. Similarly, as in Beresford and Wallcraft's (1997) observations about the dangerously narrow limitations of understanding mental health provided by psychiatry and the medical model of mental health, Richards argues that in clinical research, people get 'squashed into a medicalised narrative ... the individual and the individual's case can disappear' (Richards, 2008, p 1719); both of these are modes of silencing. Most crucially, Richards (2008, p 1720) argues that 'one way of resisting objectification is by writing about oneself.... Sometimes these narratives show that individual experience does not fit theory' and can challenge or even change the prevailing, professionally defined theory. She sees the emancipatory potential of autoethnography for social-scientific research.

Key proponents argue that autoethnograpy 'challenges canonical ways of doing research and representing others and treats research as a political, socially-just and socially-conscious act' (Ellis et al, 2011, p 1). As such, it has been used in research with and by people who are often marginalised, like black and minority ethnic people (Taylor et al, 2008), LGB people (Barton, 2010, 2011) and those who are described as 'disenfranchised', such as people who experience severe mental distress and who are subject to compulsory treatment (Muncey and Robinson, 2007). As noted earlier, Ettorre has explored the use of autoethnography as a tool for 'speaking and writing about being out in academia' and argues that it can be used as a methodology to tell her story – 'a telling creating conversations that transcends our traumas and a way of healing ourselves and others' (Ettorre, 2010, p 295). Again, the theme of the wider impact of individual narratives and their potential to create solidarity and a collective understanding is clear in Ettorre's approach for LGB people. Other LGB scholars have posited the idea that autoethnography is consistent with and can be fruitfully used alongside reflexivity and queer theory in research. Adams and Holman Jones (2011, p 111, original emphasis) write that:

> *The autoethnographic* means sharing politicised, practical and cultural stories that resonate with others and motivating these others to share theirs; bearing witness together.... *The queer* means making conversations about harmful situations go, working to improve the world one person, one family, one classroom, conference, essay at a time.

Therefore, it appears that autoethnography can be used as a tool for inquiry by LGB people who have experienced mental distress and the psychiatric system to explore and mobilise their experiences, create new collective knowledge and produce research that draws upon and is 'applicable to lived realities' (Adam and Holman Jones, 2011, p 111).

Purely personal narratives are seen as one of the more controversial forms of autoethnographic research, with critics warning of a high risk of self-indulgence and narcissism, a lack of rigour, and an over-reliance on aesthetics (Ellis et al, 2011). However, defenders of the methodology point out that this is an attempt to maintain a false dichotomy between 'art and science' and there are other approaches to autoethnography that are scientifically rigorous: 'autoethnographers believe research can be rigorous, theoretical and analytical *and* emotional, therapeutic, and inclusive of personal and social phenomena' (Ellis et al, 2011, p 11, original emphasis). Similar defence of the rigour of user and survivor research has had to be made by leaders in the field, such as Rose and others, who point out that all research has a 'standpoint' but only some research is transparent about that or actively uses standpoint knowledge as part of the research (Rose, 2008; Tew et al, 2006).

One of the approaches to a 'rigorous' form of autoethnography can be aligned with some of my own practice in creating 'encapsulating' accounts of LGB mental health that draw on personal narrative, research data and clinical practice models: 'Layered accounts often focus on the author's experience alongside data, abstract analysis and relevant literature' (Ellis et al, 2011, p 6). The idea is to 'frame existing research as a source of questions and comparisons' alongside personal narrative to create a new 'perspectival account' (Alvesson and Skoldberg, 2009), rather than to establish or measure a 'truth'. Anderson proposes an 'analytical ethnography' that could be useful for framing rigorous user and survivor research. He characterises it as research 'in which the researcher is 1) a full member in the research group or setting 2) visible as such a member in published texts 3) committed to developing theoretical understandings of broader social phenomena' (Anderson, 2006, p 373), which could certainly be said of many of the contributing survivor researchers who describe their work, experiences, epistemologies and methodologies books, such as *This is survivor research* (Sweeney et al, 2009).

Expanding on Anderson's proposals, Vyran (2006, p 408) argues that:

> value as an analytical product is more appropriately determined by usefulness to others – does the work help us better understand or explain other people, experiences, and/ or contexts? does [sic] it contribute to collective knowledge in some way? – rather [sic] than by effective mimicking of a methodological strategy that is more widely accepted at this point in time or by the size of its sample.

The idea of research to make a difference to lived experience is strongly advocated by user and survivor researchers (Beresford, 2003; Sweeney et al, 2009). Vyran's description of how analytic autoethnographic works can contribute to collective knowledge mirrors Beresford's conception of how the experiential knowledge of individuals who use services can collectively create a wider knowledge base (Beresford, 2003).

## Conclusion

The explorations in this chapter were prompted by reflections on my own research practice as part of my PhD and were also motivated by a remark that some of my work could be categorised as 'autoethnographic'. During this chapter, I have discussed my own approaches to using autobiography and experiential knowledge to further understand and critique some of the research on and dominant clinical practice for LGB people with mental health problems, with self-representation being an important theme. I have considered the applicability of autoethnography to user and survivor research, particularly that by LGB people. The methodological principles and framework of autoethnography could offer an important means of capturing individual narratives and collective knowledge – the basic approach, intention and aim have many similarities to user and survivor research and it may have the potential to contribute to methodologies in the field.

To return to the idea of marginalised individual narratives and collective knowledge, one autoethnographic researcher has argued that:

> the task of life history and personal narrative is not merely to develop a catalogue of silenced lives, as if such a creation of a catalogue is sufficient, but rather, we undertake such research to challenge the oppressive structures that create the conditions for silencing. (Tierney, 1998, p 55)

This is a core aim of user and survivor research: 'User controlled research has an important role to play here, pulling together "user knowledge" in a systematic way. In this way, groups can develop their own discourses, to set next to, and sometimes challenge, prevailing views and understandings' (Beresford, 2003, p 39). Such approaches have enormous significance for LGB people who experience mental distress, whose voices and stories have been marginalised and pathologised.

Work on the use of LGB stories as cultural resources has concluded that 'personal stories about lesbian and gay lives become strong stories when there are audiences willing to hear them ... thus they become resources for community building and political action and for shaping personal lives' (Heaphy, 2009, pp 134–5). So, LGB user and survivor research can incorporate individual experience and personal narrative, but it has the potential to become part of collective knowledge for others to draw on and add to. In this way, it can make a social contribution to the alleviation of isolation and promotion of a feeling of solidarity, as perhaps demonstrated by an email I received in response to a critical policy paper I wrote about sexuality and religion (Carr, 2008), in which the correspondent wrote:

> I read your paper on sexuality and religion a couple of years ago, and I must say parts of it really had me nodding as if I'd contributed to it myself. It affirmed so much of my own experience as a social work student, as a past service user, and I suppose as a citizen. (Tom, personal correspondence, 2011)

As Beresford has argued:

> it is possible to move from individual to collective knowledge. We can share our experience with others and relate our different interpretations and understandings of experience to each other. In this way, it becomes possible to develop knowledge which synthesises people's understandings and perspectives on their common (and varied) experience. (Beresford, 2003, p 39)

## Acknowledgements

Thanks go to my PhD supervisors, Dr Helen Cosis Brown and Professor Peter Ryan, for their support and encouragement. This chapter is written in a personal capacity and does not necessarily represent the views of the Social Care Institute for Excellence.

## References

Adams, T. and Holman Jones, S. (2011) 'Telling stories: reflexivity, queer theory and autoethnography', *Cultural Studies Critical Methodologies*, vol 11, no 2, pp 108–16.

Allison, D. (1996) *Two or three things I know for sure*, New York, NY: Plume.

Alvesson, M. and Skoldberg, K. (2009) *Reflexive methodology: new vistas for qualitative research*, London: Sage.

Anderson, L. (2006) 'Analytic autoethnography', *Journal of Contemporary Ethnography*, vol 35, no 4, pp 373–95.

Barnes, C. (1992) 'Qualitative research: valuable or irrelevant?', *Disability, Handicap and Society*, vol 7, no 2, pp 115–24.

Barnes, C. (2003) 'What a difference a decade makes: reflections on doing "emancipatory" disability research', *Disability and Society*, vol 18, no 1, pp 3–17.

Barton, B. (2010) '"Abomination" – life as a Bible Belt gay', *Journal of Homosexuality*, vol 57, no 4, pp 465–84.

Barton, B. (2011) 'My auto/ethnographic dilemma: who owns the story?', *Qualitative Sociology*, vol 34, pp 431–45.

Beresford, P. (2000) 'Service users' knowledges and social work theory: conflict or collaboration?', *British Journal of Social Work*, vol 30, no 4, pp 489–503.

Beresford, P. (2003) *It's our lives: a short theory of knowledge, distance and experience*, London: OSP for Citizen Press.

Beresford, P. and Wallcraft, J. (1997) 'Psychiatric system survivors and emancipatory research: issues, overlaps and differences', in C. Barnes and G. Mercer (eds) *Doing disability research*, Leeds: The Disability Press, pp 66–87.

Beresford, P., Nettle, M. and Perring, R. (2010) *Towards a social model of madness and distress?*, York: Joseph Rowntree Foundation.

Blasius, M. (1994) *Gay and lesbian politics: sexuality and the emergence of a new ethic*, Philadelphia, PA: Philadelphia University Press.

Bochner, A. (1994) 'Perspectives on inquiry II: theories and stories', in M. Knapp and G. Miller (eds) *Handbook of interpersonal communication*, Thousand Oaks, CA: Sage, pp 21–41.

Browne, K. and Nash, C. (2010) *Queer methods and methodologies: intersecting queer theories and social science research*, Farnham: Ashgate.

Carr, S. (2005) '"The sickness label infected everything we said": lesbian and gay perspectives on mental distress', in J. Tew (ed) *Social perspectives in mental health*, London: Jessica Kingsley, pp 168–83.

Carr, S. (2008) 'Sexuality and religion: a challenge for diversity strategies in UK social care service development and delivery', *Diversity in Health and Social Care*, vol 5, no 2, pp 113–22.

Carr, S. (2011a) '"A chance to cut is a chance to cure": self harm and self protection – a gay perspective', in P. Hafford-Letchfield and P. Dunk-West (eds) *Sexual identities and sexuality in social work: research and reflections from women in the field*, Farnham: Ashgate, pp 31–45.

Carr, S. (2011b) 'Mental health and the sexual, religious and spiritual identities of lesbian, gay, bisexual and transgender (LGBT) people', in P. Gilbert (ed) *Spirituality and mental health*, Brighton: Pavilion Publishing, pp 335–52.

Chamberlayne, P., Bornat, J. and Wengraf, T. (2000) *The turn to biographical methods in social science*, London: Routledge.

Cronin, A., Ward, R., Pugh, S., King, A. and Price, E. (2011) 'Categories and their consequences: understanding and supporting the caring relationships of older lesbian, gay and bisexual people', *International Social Work*, vol 54, no 3, pp 421–35.

Ellis, C. and Bochner, A. (2000) 'Autoethnography, personal narrative, reflexivity', in N. Denzin and Y. Lincoln (eds) *Handbook of qualitative research* (2nd edn), Thousand Oaks, CA: Sage, pp 733–68.

Ellis, C., Adams, T. and Bochner, A. (2011) 'Autoethnography: an overview forum', *Qualitative Social Research*, vol 12, no 1, pp 1–17.

Ettorre, E. (1980) *Lesbians, women and society*, London: Routledge.

Ettorre, E. (2010) 'Nuns, dykes and gendered bodies: an autoethnography of a lesbian feminist's journey through "good time" sociology', *Sexualities*, vol 13, no 3, pp 295–315.

Fenge, L. and Hicks, C. (2011) 'Hidden lives: the importance of recognising the needs and experiences of older lesbians and gay men within healthcare practice', *Diversity in Health and Care*, vol 8, no 3, pp 147–54.

Finlay, L. and Gough, B. (eds) (2003) *Reflexivity: a practical guide for researchers in health and social science*, Oxford: Blackwell.

Fish, J. (2009) 'Invisible no more? Including lesbian, gay and bisexual people in social work and social care', *Practice*, vol 21, no 1, pp 47–64.

Freud, S. (2002) *The Schreber case*, London: Penguin Classics.

Frye, M. (1983) *The politics of reality: essays in feminist theory*, New York, NY: Crossing Press.

Goodley, D. and Clough, P. (2004) 'Community projects and excluded young people: reflections on a participatory narrative approach', *International Journal of Inclusive Education*, vol 8, no 4, pp 331–51.

Green, B., Johnson, C. and Adams, A. (2001) 'Writing narrative literature reviews for peer reviewed journals: secrets of the trade', *Journal of Sports Chiropractic and Rehabilitation*, vol 15, no 1, pp 5–19.

Greenhalgh, T. and Hurwitz, B. (1998) *Narrative based medicine*, London: BMJ Books.

Hammer, B. (2010) *HAMMER! Making movies out of sex and life*, New York, NY: The Feminist Press at CUNY.

Hammer, B. and Taylor, A. (2007) 'Open your eyes: experimental filmmaker Barbara Hammer looks back on her thirty-plus years in film', *Filmmaker Magazine Winter 2007*. Available at: www.egs.edu/faculty/barbara-hammer/articles/open-your-eyes (accessed 31 May 2012).

Harding, S. (1993) Rethinking standpoint epistemology: what is "strong objectivity"?', in L. Alcoff and E. Potter (eds) *Feminist epistemologies*, New York, NY: Routledge, pp 49–82.

Heaphy, B. (2009) 'The storied, complex lives of older GLBT adults', *Journal of GLBT Family Studies*, vol 5, pp 119–38.

hooks, b. (1990a) 'Marginality as site of resistance', in R. Ferguson, M. Gever, T. Minh-ha and C. West (eds) *Out there: marginalisation and contemporary cultures*, Cambridge, MA: MIT Press, pp 341–5.

hooks, b. (1990b) *Talking back: thinking feminist, thinking black*, Boston, MA: South End.

Humphries, B. (2000) *Research in social care and social welfare: issues and debates for practice*, London: Jessica Kingsley.

Lorde, A. (2001) *Zami: a new spelling of my name – a biomythography*, Freedom, CA: The Crossing Press.

McLaurin, S. (2003) 'Homophobia: an autoethnographic story', *The Qualitative Report*, vol 8, no 3, pp 481–6.

Merril, B. and West, L. (2009) *Using biographical methods in social research*, London: Sage.

Muncey, T. (2006) 'Mixing art and science: a bridge over troubled waters or a bridge too far?', *Journal of Research in Nursing*, vol 11, no 13, pp 223–33.

Muncey, T. and Robinson, R. (2007) 'Extinguishing the voices: living with the ghost of the disenfranchised', *Journal of Psychiatric and Mental Health Nursing*, vol 14, pp 79–84.

Oliver, M. (1996) *Understanding disability, from theory to practice*, London: Macmillan.

Petersen, A. (2011) 'Research with individuals labeled "other": reflections on the research process', *Disability and Society*, vol 26, no 3, pp 293–305.

Plummer, K. (1995) *Telling sexual stories: power, change and social worlds*, London: Routledge.

Richards, R. (2008) 'Writing the othered self: autoethnography and the problem of objectification in writing about illness and disability', *Qualitative Health Research*, vol 18, no 12, pp 1717–28.

Roberts, G. (2000) 'Narrative and severe mental illness: what place do stories have in an evidence-based world?', *Advances in Psychiatric Treatment*, vol 6, pp 432–441.

Rose, D. (2004) 'Telling different stories: user involvement in mental health research', *Research Policy and Planning*, vol 22, no 2, pp 23–30.

Rose, D. (2008) 'Service user produced knowledge (editorial)', *Journal of Mental Health*, vol 17, no 3, pp 447–51.

Rose, D., Wykes, T., Bindman, J. and Fleischmann, P. (2005) 'Information, consent and perceived coercion: patients' perspectives on electroconvulsive therapy', *British Journal of Psychiatry*, vol 186, pp 54–9.

Schreber, D.P. (2000) *Memoirs of my nervous illness*, New York, NY: New York Review of Books/Harvard University Press.

Shakespeare, P., Atkinson, D. and French, S. (1993) *Reflecting on research practice: issues in health and social welfare*, Buckingham: Open University Press.

Smith, G., Bartlett, A. and King, M. (2004) 'Treatments of homosexuality in Britain since the 1950s – an oral history: the experience of patients', *British Medical Journal*, DOI: 10.1136/bmj.37984.442419. EE (published 29 January).

Stanley, L. (1990) *Feminist praxis: research, theory and epistemology in feminist sociology*, London: Routledge.

Stanley, L. (1993) 'Auto/biography', *Sociology: special issue*, vol 27, no 1, pp 41–52.

Stone, E. and Priestley, M, (1996) 'Parasites, pawns and partners: disability research and the role of non-disabled researchers', *British Journal of Sociology*, vol 47, no 4, pp 699–716.

Sweeney, A., Beresford, P., Faulkner, A., Nettle, M. and Rose, D. (eds) (2009) *This is survivor research*, Ross-on-Wye: PCCS Books, pp 22–37.

Taylor, J., Lehan Mackin, M. and Oldenburg, A. (2008) 'Engaging racial autoethnography as teaching tool for womanist inquiry', *Advances in Nursing Science*, vol 31, no 4, pp 342–55.

Tew, J., Gould, N., Abankwa, D., Barnes, H., Beresford, P., Carr, S., Copperman, J., Ramon, S., Rose, D., Sweeney, A. and Woodward, L. (2006) *Values and methodologies for social research in mental health*, London: NIMHE/SCIE/SPN.

Tierney, W. (1998) 'Life's history's history: subjects foretold', *Qualitative Inquiry*, vol 4, no 1, pp 49–70.

Tolich, M. (2010) 'A critique of current practice: ten foundational guidelines for autoethnographers', *Qualitative Health Research*, vol 20, no 12, pp 1599–610.

Trotter, J., Brogatzki, L., Duggan, L., Foster, L. and Levie, J. (2006) 'Revealing disagreement and discomfort through auto-ethnography and personal narrative', *Qualitative Social Work*, vol 5, no 3, pp 369–88.

Truman, C. (2000) 'New social movements and social research', in C. Humphries, D. Merten and B. Truman (eds) *Research and inequality*, London: UCL Press, pp 24–37.

Turner, M. and Beresford, P. (2005) *User-controlled research: its meanings and potential*, Eastleigh: INVOLVE.

Uotinen, J. (2011) 'Senses, bodily knowledge and autoethnography: unbeknown knowledge from an ICU experience', *Qualitative Health Research*, vol 21, no 10, pp 1307–15.

Vickers, M. (2007) 'Autoethnography as sensemaking: a story of bullying', *Culture and Organisation*, vol 13, no 3, pp 223–37.

Vyran, K. (2006) 'Expanding analytic autoethnography and enhancing its potential', *Journal of Contemporary Ethnography*, vol 35, no 4, pp 405–9.

Wilkins, P. (2000) 'Storytelling as research', in B. Humphries (ed) *Research in social care and social welfare: issues for debate and practice*, London: Jessica Kingsley, pp 144–54.

Winterson, J. (2001) *Oranges are not the only fruit*, London: Vintage.

Witkin, S. (2000) 'Writing social work', *Social Work*, vol 45, no 5, pp 1–9.

# ELEVEN

# Alternative futures for service user involvement in research

*Hugh McLaughlin*

## Introduction

This chapter will seek to raise the reader's awareness of the often taken-for-granted assumptions about the future for service user researchers. In particular, it is not assumed that there is only one potential future, but many, all of which have their own implications for both service user researchers and non-service user researchers. The chapter will begin by identifying what we mean by a service user, identifying some of the strengths and limitations of this concept, and the notion of participatory research, before highlighting the way service users have been involved in research, the differing claims made for types of service user researchers and concluding by examining potential futures for service user researchers.

It is important to state from the very beginning that I am a supporter of service user involvement in research. I firmly believe that we have traditionally missed out on an important aspect of research's potential and impoverished our understanding of research's meaning and effectiveness by failing to actively involve service users in the research process concerning issues that directly affect them.

## What does it mean to be a service user?

The notion of a service user is at first a social construction that attempts to define an identity and a relationship between those who commission or provide services and those who are the recipients of those services. It is important to note that the terms 'service user' and 'service provider' are not neutral entities and, as McDonald (2006, p 115) has rightly observed:

> The words we use to describe those who use our services are, at one level, metaphors that indicate how we conceive them.

At another level such labels operate discursively constructing both the relationship and the attendant identities of people participating in the relationship including very practical and material outcomes.

The term 'service user' was an attempt to acknowledge that those who were in receipt of welfare services had a right to have a say in the services they received or wished to receive. This new relationship sought to challenge the previous use of such terms as 'client', 'consumer', 'customer', 'expert by experience' or 'patient', all of which McLaughlin (2009b) has shown to be seriously flawed and signify different types of relationships and power differentials between professionals and those they seek to serve. The term 'service user' is not universally accepted, as Shaping Our Lives, a national service user network, has claimed that:

> The term 'service user' can be used to restrict your identity as if all you are is a passive recipient of health and welfare services. That is to say that, a service user can be seen as someone who has things 'done to them' or who quietly accepts and receives a service. This makes it seem that the most important thing about you is that you use or have used services. It ignores the other things you do and which make up you as a person. (Shaping Our Lives Network, 2003, cited in Warren, 2007, p 8)

Shaping Our Lives rightly remind us that the term 'service user' can be viewed as a homogenised label viewing the totality of a person through the prism of their service user status, neglecting the possibility that individuals may have alternative, potentially higher statuses as a mother, school governor, magistrate or even as an academic! The term 'service user' can also be criticised for neglecting those who, for whatever reason, may be entitled to a service but fail to access such services for fear of stigma, what the Sainsbury Centre for Mental Health (2002, p 8) have described as 'a circle of fear'. In particular, they highlighted the position of black and minority ethnic groups avoiding mental health services for fear of racism. Focusing just on service users raises the possibility that we may be ignoring the prospect that services may not be meeting the needs of those for whom they were designed.

A more recent aspect of this critique has been the development of personalised care (DH, 2007) and, in particular, direct payments, whereby those we previously termed 'service users' become recipient of funds from which they are able to employ a personal carer or commission other services. It thus becomes rather difficult to describe such individuals as service users and represents a potential fracture line for the future of the term 'service user'. In the future, we are likely to need to find new terminology, but for the present, 'service user' is the best term available, signifying that there are those who are service providers or commissioners and those who use those services. For the purposes of this chapter, a service user may be considered as someone who is on the receiving end or eligible to receive health and social care services. It should also be remembered that those who are service commissioners or providers may also be service users, while, as we will note later, there are also academic researchers who are service users or service users who are academics. The two terms are not mutually exclusive.

At this stage of the chapter, I should declare that I am currently not a service user but may well be in the future. As such, it is possible for all of us to recognise that we all have a stake in this debate to ensure that any services that are developed and provided are ones that we would all wish to use. This leads us onto the involvement of service users in research.

## Involving service users in research

In working with children and young people, Christensen and Prout (2002) have identified a useful typology of four different models of service user involvement. These models move from viewing service users as objects to subjects to social actors to active participants. Traditionally, service user involvement in research was restricted to being the objects of research. People with learning disabilities have traditionally been measured, labelled and categorised. This view has often been associated with quantitative research approaches, where the research is carried out by a researcher in an objective manner irrespective of the research objects' views or experiences.

The second approach sees the service users as subjects and, as such, brings them to the forefront of the research process. This represents a much more service user-centred approach, but potentially has shortcomings in that it is often tempered by the researcher's assessment of the service user's ability, competency or maturity. This is often linked to the Kantian notion of respect for persons. Downie and Telfer (1969) view the essential ingredients of respect for persons as being capable of rational thought and acting with intent. Such a perspective can have major implications for service user research, where service users are often identified as vulnerable, or at risk. This can be particularly relevant when considering the position of those suffering from a mental illness or those with Alzheimer's disease, not to mention the situation of children and young people. In applying Downie and Telfer's prescription, it is possible to argue that those with a mental illness are 'lapsed persons', those with Alzheimer's as 'ex-persons' and children and young people as 'potential persons', thus allowing the researcher to decide what is best, irrespective of the views of the service user. This view has been challenged, particularly in sociology, where it has been argued that it is important to view children and young people as 'beings not becomings' (Qvortrup et al, 1994, p 2, cited in Clark, 2004, p 142). Clark and Moss (2011) have also shown that it is possible to work with notions of competency when researching the perspectives of children under five years old using the mosaic approach, whose principles and creativity is potentially transferable to other marginalised groups.

The third approach views service users as social actors and not merely as passive recipients of services. This perspective acknowledges that service users are not just there to be 'done to' or shaped by their external world, but act on the world, both being shapers as well as being shaped. In this perspective, service users are viewed as possessing 'agency' and are thus able to make meaningful and autonomous choices to effect change in both their and others' lives.

The fourth approach is a special case of the third approach and views service users as active participants or collaborators in the research process to co-produce new knowledge. In co-production, Needham and Carr (2009) suggest that both service user researchers and traditional researchers are empowered to work together, emphasising that both have skills, expertise, knowledges and experiences to bring to the research process – 'working with rather than doing to' – to produce an effective outcome. For the purposes of this chapter, this begs the question as to the quantity and quality of involvement that needs to occur before it is possible to suggest that the co-production can be viewed as meaningful.

It could also be suggested that service user-controlled research, which is discussed in the next section, could be conceptualised as the natural extension of Christensen and Prout's typology, where service users are in control of the whole process.

## Service user involvement in the research continuum

Probably the best known continuum of involvement is Arnstein's (1971) ladder of citizen participation, which was also translated to children and young people by Hart (1992). Hanley et al (2004) usefully reduced

Arnstein's eight rungs to three: consultation, collaboration and service user control. Hanley et al (2004), however, neglected Arnstein's negative examples of service user involvement that can be captured in the notion of tokenism. Tokenism may occur either intentionally or unintentionally. Intentional tokenism may occur where a researcher seeks to involve service users to merely tick a box in a research application form to satisfy a research commissioner. Unintentional tokenism may occur when the researcher, through their lack of understanding, acts in ways to exclude service users by, for example, holding meetings at inaccessible venues, being unable to pay expenses promptly or using language and acronyms that exclude rather than include. For these reasons, it is important to *acknowledge* that not all service user involvement can be viewed as inherently positive.

Hanley et al's (2004) first point on the continuum is consultation and refers to asking service users to help inform decision-making, which may or may not be influenced by the consultation. Consultation is safe for researchers as it implies no mandate for action and this has led to complaints of 'consultationitis' or 'consultation overload' by black and minority ethnic elders, who see nothing happening to their conditions in response to the consultations (Butt and O'Neill, 2004).

Collaboration, the next step in the continuum, exists in the middle ground between consultation and service user-controlled research. In the collaborative approach, there is an assumption of ongoing involvement in the research, with an awareness that it would be possible for the service user to indicate how their involvement in the research has made a difference. Collaboration can take many forms, for example, being a member of an advisory group, establishing the research questions, interviewing other service users, data analysis, writing up and dissemination; all or any combination of these potentially represents collaboration. It is probably unfair, as it is with any other research team, to expect service user researchers or other researchers to contribute to all aspects of the research. Similarly, different service user researchers should be able to contribute to different aspects of the research process. The reason why most research is conducted within teams is to ensure that we have the requisite experience and skills required to fully address the research question.

We now move on to service user-controlled research, which differs from collaborative research in that it is assumed that the locus of power is not shared, but is located firmly in the hands of service users. Evans and Jones (2004, p 8) identify the key elements of service user-controlled research as: 'about service users determining the research focus, the research process, the interpretation of the findings, and the conclusions to be drawn for practice and policy'.

Turner and Beresford (2005), in a review of service user-controlled research, identified a split between those who felt that you could only have service user-controlled research where all aspects of the research were undertaken by service users, and others who viewed this as too pure a principle and felt that what mattered was that the service users had control of the process and could commission researchers to work to their specifications and that they maintained control of the research process and products. It does, however, suggest that service user-controlled research remains a contested arena.

In this section, we have considered four different levels of service user involvement in research: tokenism, consultation, collaboration and service user-controlled research. All except the first may be appropriate at different times with service user co-researchers and will depend on the nature of the research question and the skills of the service user researchers. In any research project, it may be appropriate at times for service users to be consulted, be collaborated with or even to take the lead. It should also be acknowledged that involving service user researchers meaningfully as co-researchers is not only a technical question, but also a political one concerned with issues of citizenship, democracy, social justice and inclusion.

## Participatory research

Participatory research is a contested concept; however, Cresswell (2003, p 11) captures four of the key tenets of participatory research when he notes that participatory action:

- is recursive or dialectic and is focused on bringing about change in practice;
- is focused on helping individuals free themselves from constraints found in the media, in language, in work procedures and in relations of power in educational settings;
- is emancipatory in that it helps unshackle people, from the constraints of irrational and unjust structures that limit self-development and self-determination; and
- is practical and collaborative because it is enquiry completed 'with' others rather than 'on' or 'to' others. In this spirit, advocacy/ participatory authors engage the participants as active collaborators in their inquiries.

From these characteristics, it can easily by seen why such approaches are favoured by those involved in service user research. Research becomes not merely a process, but also a mandate for challenging injustice and inequality, addressing oppression, and promoting empowerment and change. As Glasby and Beresford (2006) note, research only becomes justified when it promotes change. Participatory approaches have their roots in feminist perspectives, racialised discourses, critical theory, queer theory and disability inquiry, which have all sought to challenge mainstream views and discourses (McLaughlin, 2012).

Participatory research sees the involvement of service users in research as both a right of being a citizen and a feature of improved research quality. Smith (2012) argues that there are two distinct, but overlapping, sets of questions to be considered if we wish to term service user research as participatory research. In particular, he highlights issues concerning the extent and integrity of the participation and practical considerations. The first set of questions consider which aspects (if not all) of the research the service user researcher has been involved in: what roles in the research did they take? What decisions and informed choices did they make? Did the research achieve what they wanted? And did they retain control over the dissemination and subsequent use of the research? The second set of questions consider identifying in what ways the research had been enhanced through participation: how might it have been compromised, for example, limitations in methods used? How did the participatory approach support ethical practice? And how were ethical challenges negotiated, for example, sharing of personal details?

From Smith's (2012) analysis, it could be suggested that total participation can only be an aspirational goal where service users are working as co-researchers. Even the experience of service user-controlled research, as previously noted by Turner and Beresford (2005), may not achieve a pure model of participatory research. This is not to say that participatory approaches should not be pursued, but that it may be more appropriate to aspire to create participative ownership of particular aspects of the research process in some cases. It also begs the question of where the tipping point sits for something to be legitimately recognised as participatory research.

## Differing types of service user researchers

McLaughlin (2010) raises the question as to whether a service user researcher or co-researcher has to be in receipt of the services they are seeking to research. There are at least three differing aspects to this: as a direct, indirect or alternative researcher. The first of these, the direct, refers to service users who are currently in receipt of services from the service provider under research or who have recently been in receipt of services. However, it remains unclear how recent this experience should be; certainly, if they only stopped receiving the service three months ago, it would appear reasonable to describe them as direct service user researchers, but is this the same for someone who has not been in receipt of services for three years or, say, 13 years? At what point does it, if ever, become implausible to claim to be a service user researcher when you have not been in receipt of the services under investigation. This is pertinent as it is hoped that new developments and research will have contributed to new modes and types of service delivery.

The indirect service user researcher captures the notion that a disability service user in the north-west could be a research team member investigating disability services in the south-east. They are not in receipt of the services under investigation but they do have personal experience of being in receipt of similar services by a different provider in a different geographical location. Thus, while their experiences of service delivery are likely to be similar to those they are researching, they will not be exactly the same.

The third type of service user is the alternative researcher. This involves those who are service users, or have been service users in one service context, for example, breast cancer services, who are part of a research team researching another aspect of welfare service provision, say, mental health services. As McLaughlin (2010, p 1594) notes:

> In this type of scenario the added insight of being a service user is mediated and diluted by their lack of knowledge of the field and individual nuances within the service user experiences under investigation. You would not normally expect to give service users who are blind preferred treatment in a research study investigating the experience of those using services for the deaf.

This is not to deny that we have people who are both deaf and blind or who have breast cancer and suffer mental illness. It does, however, begin to raise an issue that is often overlooked in the literature. There appears to be a general assumption that service user experiences are either the same, or similar enough, to be able to justify a claim of privileged insight and understanding not only for the services a service user may have experienced, but also for all welfare services. This assumption of similarity of service user experience is a particularly fragile claim.

It could be claimed that those with a physical disability may have a differing relationship to medical services: they may view them as an opportunity to reduce their dependency through medical intervention, for example, cochlear implants or groundbreaking eye surgery, while mental health service users may view medical intervention as controlling and negative. Similarly, black feminist researchers have deliberately distanced themselves from their white colleagues as their primary marker for difference was racism, not patriarchy (Payne, 2005). Evans and Banton (2001, pp 2–3) also note that 'attitudes towards "race" within white organisations and disability within black organisations have created major barriers to the involvement of black people'.

Begum (2006) goes on to claim that the service user movement is just as likely to be racist as any other part of British society. Barnes and Mercer (2006) also remind us that it is absurd to believe that just because someone is disabled, it necessarily implies that they will have a natural affinity with other disabled people. Previously, Barnes (1992) had highlighted other intersecting identity markers, including class, education, employment and life experience. To these, we could also add ethnicity, gender, disability, sexual orientation and so on. The matching of service researchers to those whom they may wish to research can thus be seen as highly problematic.

Second, welfare services are not randomly accessed by all parts of society. We know that there is an over-representation of black people and mixed-race people in compulsory mental health admissions. The Healthcare Commission (2005) survey *Count us in* found that black or mixed-race people represented almost 10% of mental health patients but that 44% of black people were compulsorily detained under a statutory order and were twice as likely to be referred to mental health services by the police or courts than white mental health patients.

While the two issues just raised do not invalidate the potential of service user researchers, it does remind us of the dangers of over- or under-claiming service user researcher status as a sole criterion for authentic research results.

## Alternative service user researcher futures

In the last section, we discussed differing types of service user researchers that we will now build on to look at alternative service user research trajectories for the future. Before examining potential trajectories, it is worth noting that we are now at an exciting time for service user researchers. As mentioned at the beginning, we now have a number of academics, for example, Professor Peter Beresford (a contributor to this volume) or Professor Colin Barnes, who acknowledge their service user status, often identifying with the service user community more than the academic community. Other academics, like Anne Wilson (Wilson and Beresford, 2000), have used a pseudonym for fear of prejudice or discrimination from their employer as result of their service user status. Assuming that academics are also representative of a cross-section of society, there are many more academics who either do not feel that it is significant enough for their work to acknowledge being a service user or, like Anne Wilson, do not feel able to acknowledge this part of their identity for fear of prejudice. At the other end of the spectrum, we are seeing a number of service user researchers successfully completing PhDs, like Dr Patsy Staddon, the editor of this volume. More recently, I interviewed a mental health service user for a PhD studentship. Thus, we are seeing more academics willing to acknowledge their joint identities and service users who are using their experience of research to develop new identities. On top of this, groups like INVOLVE (www.invo.org.uk) are funded by the National Institute of Health Research (NIHR) to promote patient and service user involvement in health, public health and social care research, with Dame Sally Davies (2009, p 4), when Director General of Research and Development in the Department of Health, declaring that: 'I have always taken the view that public involvement in research should be the rule not the exception. It is fundamental to ensure high quality research that brings real benefits for patients, the public and the NHS.' Alongside this, we also have more academics, like myself, who actively support this type of research and seek to tease out both its potential and its limitations.

In realising the potential of service user involvement in research, we need to consider the issue of training for service users who have previously had no experience in research. Lockey et al (2004) found that service user research training was essential in ensuring service user research involvement in research and led to benefits in terms of self-confidence, self-esteem and personal development. Many projects provide project-specific training and it is unethical to ask service user researchers to undertake tasks that they have not been appropriately prepared for. As noted earlier, a number of service user researchers are undertaking academic research training and will thus be able to contribute more fully to research projects. The point here is that, like any research team member, service user researchers should only be asked to undertake research roles that they have had training for and that are within their competence.

As more service users become research-active and take part in more research projects, it becomes a contested and contestable point to consider whether there reaches a point whereby service user researchers becomes more like traditional researchers than service user researcher.s In other words, at what point, if at all, do service user researchers become more valued for their research expertise as opposed to their service user experience? In an ideal world, we would seek to harness both for the purpose of the research. However, balancing the two may be easier to say than to do. Individuals may find that with more exposure to research projects, one of the two predilections becomes the more dominant. If this is the service user experience, this is not a problem, but if it is the researcher expertise, does this begin to suggest they have begun to 'go native' and have less to offer from their experience of being a service user?

At this stage, it is important to remember that service user research is not inherently benign and, as Beresford (2002) acknowledges, service user involvement contains the potential for both liberation and regression. While interest in service user research has been growing and has been increasingly required by government and other funding bodies, this does not mean that the essence of service user involvement in research has not been marginalised, co-opted or just implemented in tokenistic ways. Service user involvement in research is inherently political in that it is not concerned with neutral or objective 'fact-finding' but exists to improve service users' life and service experiences, challenging traditional ways of working, promoting social change and supporting the empowerment of service users.

At the regressive end of the scale, service user researchers could continue to be used in tokenistic ways, added onto research proposals to tick the right boxes but having no influence over the research process or its outcomes. Service user researchers are 'included' in research teams to massage the research teams' service user credentials and external image. Or, it may be done in such a way as to ensure that the service user researchers are left with the jobs no one else wants or are only given the most menial of tasks to undertake. An example of this might be where service user researchers are taken on as interviewers but are asked to administer closed-question surveys on service user experiences based on a set of questions that they have had no input on. A result of this is not only poorer research, but also the likelihood that service user researchers will drop out of research teams and refuse to get involved in research in the future. Such an approach is likely to contaminate the field for others.

At the other end of the scale is a version of standpoint service user-controlled research that views the only legitimate type of research in relation to service provision or service user experiences as solely that carried out by service users themselves. This perspective privileges the experiential knowledge of service users as the only authentic perspective on services. It is only they, not service providers, managers, social policy experts or even family members, who experience policy and practice from the receiving end and thus only they who can truly understand the impact and intended and unintended consequences of a treatment or intervention. This standpoint position risks replacing the tyranny of traditional academic research practice with the tyranny of service user-controlled research that eschews other perspectives and other experiences on the grounds that they are not the experience of service users and thus, by definition, must be of an inferior status. Service user researchers may be in a better position to understand some aspects of practice but this is a different type of claim to saying that there is only one authentic view. As Hammersley (1995, p 51) has commented:

> Whilst we must recognize that people in different social locations may have divergent perspectives giving them distinctive insights, it is not clear why we should believe in the implausible claim that some category of people has privileged access whilst others are blinded by ideology.

Hammersley (1995) helpfully acknowledges that in our social location as a service user researcher, non-service user researcher, practitioner, manager or policy officer, we all have similar and differing perspectives on service provision and that it is only by capturing all these stakeholder perspectives that we can begin to understand these issues holistically. This is not to suggest that we may need to look for alternative ways of interweaving the differing knowledge claims, promoting a dialogue that potentially has great learning for all. Nolan et al (2007, p 190) capture this dilemma when they write:

> If we accept that differing types of knowledge and expertise contribute to a full understanding, then no one has privileged 'insider' knowledge, but everyone has differing knowledge from which everyone can learn. Herein lies the nub of the issue.

This leads on to our third potential future for service user researchers, which is for service user researchers to be co-researchers in research teams or service user-controlled research, making a full and valid contribution to health and social care research. In order for this to happen, there are a number of prerequisites, including funding for service user involvement in research, more research on outcomes, a rapprochement with other modes of knowledge production and a clearer understanding of the benefits and costs of service user involvement in research.

In this period of austerity, it remains difficult for any researchers to obtain sufficient funding. It is even more difficult for non-service user researchers to secure sufficient funding for collaborative research involving service user researchers and it remains even more difficult again for user-controlled organisations to secure funding in their own right (Turner and Beresford, 2005). If we are to ensure that service user research becomes an integral part of the evidence base for policy and practice, it requires proper funding.

One of the biggest challenges for service user involvement in research concerns the issue of outcomes and impact. Too often, research reports and articles involving service users as researchers have been evaluated in terms of the nature of the involvement, with insufficient attention being paid to the outcomes. Research contains both a process and task. If the process is seen as positive, service user researchers will feel that they have done well irrespective of whether the research makes a difference or not. Conversely, if the research task is completed, service user researchers may feel happy that they have made a difference but the experience has been so poor that they will not wish to engage in research again. The question of process also reminds us of Barnes and Mercer's (2006) previous comments about not assuming that just because someone is a service user, they will necessarily be sympathetic to other service users. In this context, we should also be mindful that not all non-service user researchers will be good at working with service user researchers. This type of research is not suitable for every researcher, and if they wish to work in this way, researchers have to be able to develop a skill set that includes expertise in community work, group work, expressing themselves succinctly in plain English and being able to empathise with their co-researchers.

If both the process and task completion are poor, service user researchers are likely not to wish to be involved in research again and will probably counsel other service users to do the same. If, on the other hand, both the process and the achievement of the task are experienced as positive, this becomes a win–win scenario for both the research and the research team. In such circumstances, whether the service user researchers decide to become involved in future research projects as researchers is to some extent immaterial, as they are more likely to encourage others to become researchers or to be research participants given their positive experience and ability to be able to identify changes that came from their research experience.

## Conclusions and final thoughts

Involving service users, either as co-researchers or as researchers in service user-controlled research, has developed significantly in recent years. It has now reached the stage whereby if it is to continue to develop, we must become more rigorous and critical of both its processes and impact. We need to ensure that service user involvement in research remains honest, being able to openly discuss and debate what it can and cannot do (McLaughlin, 2010). Some service user researchers are, or were previously, academically qualified, or are members of service user-controlled research teams, and this may open up a new future as service user researchers. For others who work on service provision areas or with service user groups with whom they have no affiliation, the future may be as members of alternative research teams bidding against other non-service user researchers for research contracts.

For a third group, there is a clear need for all of us to remain vigilant and to challenge the situations where we find that the involvement of service user researchers is tokenistic, a mechanistic box-ticking exercise at best and a corruption of research at worst. Such an approach is unlikely to encourage service users or those with whom they are in contact with to continue their involvement in research.

There will also be a fourth group who no longer wish to be involved as co-researchers but who benefited from the experience in terms of confidence-building, esteem and employability. For this group, the involvement in research will have been part of life's rich tapestry.

We all have a stake in the future health of service user research and in making sure that health and social care policy and practice can capitalise on the experiences of those who have been in receipt of services. This has to be done in a way that allows us to amalgamate the differing research traditions and research perspectives to have as complete a picture as possible of the intent, experience and impact of policy and practice. After all, we are all potential recipients of that policy and practice.

### References

Arnstein, S. (1971) 'A ladder of citizen participation', *Journal of the Royal Planning Institute*, vol 35, no 4, pp 216–24.

Barnes, C. (1992) 'Qualitative research: valuable or irrelevant?', *Disability, Handicap and Society*, vol 7, no 2, pp 115–24.

Barnes, C. and Mercer, G. (2006) *Independent futures: creating user-led disability services in a disabling society*, Bristol: The Policy Press.

Begum, N. (2006) *Doing it for themselves: participation and black and minority service users*, London: SCIE/REU.

Beresford, P. (2002) 'User involvement in research and evaluation: liberation or regulation', *Social Policy and Society*, vol 1, no 2, pp 95–106.

Butt, J. and O'Neill, A. (2005) *'Let's move on': Black and Minority Ethnic older people's views on research findings*, York: Joseph Rowntree Foundation.

Christensen, P. and Prout, A. (2002) 'Working with ethical symmetry in social research with children', *Childhood*, vol 9, no 4, pp 477–97.

Clark, A. (2004) 'The mosaic approach and research with young children', in S. Fraser, V. Lewis, S. Ding, M. Kellett and C. Robinbson (eds) *The reality of research with children and young people*, London: Sage in association with the Open University Press, pp 142–56.

Clark, A. and Moss, P. (2011) *Listening to young children: the mosaic approach*, London: NCB.

Cresswell, J.W. (2003) *Research design: Qualitative, quantitative and mixed method approaches*, London: Sage.

Davies, S.C. (2009) 'Foreword', in K. Staley (ed) *Exploring impact: public involvement in the NHS, public health and social care research*, Eastleigh: INVOLVE, p 3.

DH (Department of Health) (2007) *Putting people first: a shared vision and commitment to the transformation of adult social care*, London: Stationery Office.

Downie, R.S. and Telfer, E. (1969) *Respect for persons*, London: Allen and Unwin.

Downie, R.S. and Telfer, E. (1980) *Caring and curing: a philosophy of medicine and social work*, London: Methuen.

Evans, C. and Jones, R. (2004) 'Engagement and empowerment, research and empowerment', *Research, Policy and Planning*, vol 22, no 2, pp 5–13.

Evans, R. and Banton, M. (2001) *Learning from experience: involving black disabled people in shaping services*, Warwickshire: Council of Disabled People Warwickshire.

Glasby, J. and Beresford, P. (2006) 'Who knows best? Evidence-based practice and the service user contribution', *Critical Social Policy*, vol 22, no 3, pp 223–31.

Hammersley, M. (1995) *The politics of social research*, London: Sage.

Hanley, B., Bradburn, J., Barnes, M., Evans, C., Goodare, H., Kelston, M., Kent, A., Oliver, S., Thomas, S. and Wallcraft, J. (2004) *Involving the public in NHS, public health and social care research: briefing notes for researchers*, Eastleigh: INVOLVE.

Hart, R. (1992) 'Children's participation from tokenism to citizenship', Innocenti Essays, No 4, Florence, Italy, UNICEF.

Healthcare Commission (2005) *Count us in: the results of the national census of inpatients in mental health hospitals and facilities in England and Wales*, London: Healthcare Commission.

Lockey, R., Sitzia, J., Gillingham, T., Millyard, T., Miller, C., Ahmed, S., Beales, A., Bennet, C., Parfoot, S., Sigrist, J. and Worthing and Southlands Hospitals NHS Trust (2004) *Training for service user involvement in health and social care research: a study of training provision and participants' experiences (the TRUE project)*, Worthing: Worthing and Southlands Hospitals NHS Trust.

McDonald, C. (2006) *Challenging social work: the context of practice*, Basingstoke: Palgrave Macmillan.

McLaughlin, H. (2009) 'What's in a name: "client", "patient", "customer", "consumer", "expert by experience", "service user" – what's next?', *British Journal of Social Work*, vol 39, no 6, pp 1101–17.

McLaughlin, H. (2010) 'Keeping service user involvement in research honest', *British Journal of Social Work*, vol 40, no 5, pp 1591–608.

McLaughlin, H. (2012) *Understanding social work research* (2nd edn), London: Sage.

Needham, C. and Carr, S. (2009) *SCIE research briefing 31: co-production: an emerging evidence base for adult social care transformation*, London: SCIE.

Nolan, M., Hanson, E., Grant, G. and Keady, J. (2007) 'Conclusions: realizing authentic participatory enquiry', in M. Nolan, G. Hanson, G. Grant and J. Keady (eds) *User participation in health and social care research*, Maidenhead: Open University Press, pp 183–202.

Payne, M. (2005) *Modern social work theory*, Basingstoke: Palgrave Macmillan.

Qvortrup, J., Bardy, M., Sgritta, G. and Wintersberger, H. (eds) *Childhood matters*, Vienna: European Centre

Sainsbury Centre for Mental Health (2002) *Circles of fear: a review of the relationship between mental health service users and African and Caribbean communities*, London: Sainsbury Centre for Mental Health.

Shaping Our Lives (2003) What do we mean by 'service user'? http://www.shapingourlives.org.uk/definitions.html, accessed 10 July 2011

Smith, R. (2012) 'Why participatory research? Exploring principles and practice', in J. Fleming and T. Boeck (eds) *Involving children and young people in health and social care research*, Abingdon: Routledge, pp 28–37.

Turner, M. and Beresford, P. (2005) *What user controlled research means, and what it can do*, Eastleigh: INVOLVE.

Warren, J. (2007) *Service user and carer participation in social work*, Exeter: Learning Matters.

Wilson, A. and Beresford, P. (2000) 'Anti-oppressive practice: emancipation or appropriation?', *British Journal of Social Work*, vol 30, no 5, pp 553–74.

# TWELVE

# Brief reflections

*Patsy Staddon*

For me, the most important aspect of this book is that it contextualises service user research, experiential knowledge and autoethnography. It also moves the narrative of service user experience and involvement forward, interrogating how identity shapes knowledge production. This knowledge may be used sensitively and with moral intent, promoting greater understanding, fairer distribution of resources and service user empowerment (Beresford and Evans, 1999). Silencing and social exclusion are addressed by several of the writers – by Middleton (Chapter Two) and Carr (Chapter Ten), in particular – leading to an impoverishment of knowledge (Beresford and Boxall, Chapter Six; Lewis, Chapter Seven; Staddon, Chapter Eight). Systematic investigation of our own knowledge, as Sweeney (Chapter One) has said, offers the opportunity of addressing the 'politics of recognition' and social injustice described by Lewis in Chapter Seven.

At the same time, we must ensure that we do not bring some of the prejudices and learnt behaviours of an unjust society with us (Pollard and Evans, Chapter Four), whether these involve racism, homophobia or simply a lust for power (Staddon, 2012, pp 8–9). This is a trap into which service users and service user researchers may also fall. We have emerged from a society that has dealt us prejudice and injustice, but we are still creatures of that society (Goffman, 1971 [1959]) and may bring with us new power structures and 'iron cages' (Courpasson and Clegg, 2006), an outcome sometimes seen as inevitable (Dahl, 1971) and even sometimes as having 'unexpected validity' (Courpasson, 2004, p 335).

A further danger is that existing power structures will be boosted by some kinds of service user research involvement, a possibility considered in this book by Lewis (Chapter Seven) and elsewhere by Beresford and Boxall (2012). Our participation and involvement depends for its effectiveness on a recognition of imbalances of power, and of the need to engage collaboratively and interactively with 'involvement policies' (Lewis, Chapter Seven). Further difficulties for the development of social perspectives in research are present when service users are viewed as having brought their situation upon themselves, as in the case of alcohol and drug users (and perhaps, in the future, victims of climbing accidents, eating disorders, etc, endlessly onwards). This may even be the consensus view among service users in such groups as well as among other service users and the general public (Staddon, Chapter Eight). As long as service users who become involved in research retain such understandings about the distress and responses of themselves and of others like them, shame and stigma will continue to affect and to skew research findings at every level.

Perhaps all stakeholders should be looking into what sort of service development is desirable and what is undesirable. Middleton (Chapter Two) and McLaughlin (Chapter Eleven) are right to seek out mutualities of respect and understanding within the worlds of researcher, clinician and service user, and to recommend research approaches that reflect these values. Pollard and Evans (Chapter Four) and Gillard et al (Chapter Five) demonstrate how service user involvement in research can be done well. Perhaps we can look forward to a future of partnership, not only in care (McLaughlin, Chapter Eleven) but also in research (Pollard and Evans, Chapter Four).

It is certainly possible that before long, a whole new way of looking at what is health and what is 'unhealth' will emerge from a sociology of medicine, which convinces the medical world of the importance of the social context and sociological understanding in diagnosis and treatment (Scambler, 2012).

My own hopes are tempered by feelings similar to those of Kalathil (Chapter Nine) and Carr (Chapter Ten). There are, indeed, ways forward, and we have, indeed, come a long way from a position whereby we were routinely seen as 'subjects'. Yet, the academic establishment may still support the notion of 'hard to reach', even while it searches for a phrase that offers less of an insight into how our involvement is truly perceived; defining our position as being 'out there', still objects of scrutiny rather than partners. Perhaps, to avail ourselves of effective means to understand and thus transform the lives of service users, and of society as a whole, we will need to consider how to 'take over the factory', the means of production, rather than be consulted as to the kind of machinery it is best for others to use (Marx, 1967). May ongoing stigma and inequality continue to discriminate against a broadly based research involvement of service users from different backgrounds and with different experiences of health and 'unhealth'? If so, how valid are notions of partnership in a world where fitness to participate in society is based upon perceived and imposed criteria of 'health'?

# References

Beresford, P. and Boxall, K. (2012) 'Service users, social work education and knowledge for social work practice', *Social Work Education*, vol 31, no 2, pp 155–67.

Beresford, P. and Evans, C. (1999) 'Research and empowerment', *British Journal of Social Work*, no 29, pp 671–7.

Courpasson, D. (2004) 'Contested oligarchies. Hypotheses about the political stability of business organizations', paper presented at the Organization Science Winter Conference, Steamboat Springs, 4–8 February.

Courpasson, D. and Clegg, S. (2006) 'Dissolving the iron cages? Tocqueville, Michels, bureaucracy and the perpetuation of elite power', *Organisation*, vol 13, no 3, pp 319–43.

Dahl, R.A. (1971) *Polyarchy, participation and opposition*, New Haven, CT: Yale University Press.

Goffman, E. (1971 [1959]) *The presentation of self in everyday life*, Harmondsworth: Penguin Books.

Marx, K. (1967) *Capital* (vol 1), New York, NY: International Publishers.

Scambler, G.N. (2012) 'Contemporary theory, medical sociology and health', *Contemporary theorists and medical sociology*, London: Routledge.

Staddon, P. (2012) 'Empathy, respect, inclusivity? Service users and the research process', *Open Mind*, issue 171, March and April.

# Details of the seminar series

*Lydia Lewis*

## Researching in mental health: sociological and service user/survivor perspectives: a joint seminar series between the Survivor Researcher Network and the British Sociological Association Sociology of Mental Health Study Group

Organised by: *Lydia Lewis, Angela Sweeney, Ruth Sayers and David Armes*

*Edited version of the report presented to the Foundation for the Sociology of Health and Illness, July 2009*

The aim of this seminar series was to bridge the gap between academic sociologists of mental health and service user/survivor mental health researchers, providing opportunities for learning from one another. In this respect, it was groundbreaking and was an extremely worthwhile and successful initiative, as evidenced by the feedback reported later. In fact, the aim was more than met, with each event attracting an average of around 40 attendees spread across different organisational backgrounds, including survivor/service user organisations, academia and mental health practice. The seminars provided for attendance from all over the UK, including Scotland, and internationally, with one presenter travelling from Germany and delegates attending from France and Ireland.

Five seminars took place in total (the February seminar was cancelled due to bad weather) between January and June 2009. They were hosted free of charge at the British Library in London on the first Monday of each month, from 6pm to 8pm, and all were extremely well attended. The series began with a panel session to get debate going and then featured between two and three presentations at each, with a combination of survivor/service user and sociological presentations on each occasion (see programme, outlined later). This made for lively debate and stimulating discussion at each event. This continued informally on each occasion in order to maximise benefits for participants, including networking opportunities, and opportunities to bridge divides between delegates working in different sectors and to encourage collaborative links. This aspect of the series was particularly successful, as the feedback reported later demonstrates.

In addition to oral presentations and discussion, the seminar series encompassed the display of work from two survivor organisations: the Survivor History Group and *Recovery*. This element of the series was well appreciated and added additional opportunities for dissemination and interest for delegates.

Presentations from the seminar series will be archived on the British Sociological Association Sociology of Mental Health Study Group website (available at: www.britsoc.co.uk/medsoc/MedSocMentalHealth.aspx), while possibilities for publication of papers presented during the series will be explored. An online forum has been set up in response to demand from delegates and, in light of its success and the many benefits it accrued for those involved, some of the organisers and other participants are keen to run a second seminar series. Acknowledging the extremely worthwhile nature of the initiative, the British Sociological Association has offered to support such future events, which contribute towards its 'public sociology' agenda.

In the remainder of this report, we present the programme of the seminar series, followed by some of the feedback from delegates. We would like to thank the Foundation for the Sociology of Health and Illness for supporting the initiative, and also the British Library for their support in providing the venue and funding a wine reception on the closing evening. Thanks as well to the British Sociological Association for doing such an excellent job in providing administrative support and publicity materials.

**Programme**

| 12 January 2009 | Panel session 'Mental health research by and with service-users/survivors: opportunities and barriers'. Chair: Professor Peter Beresford, Centre for Citizen Participation, Brunel University. Speakers: Professor George Szmukler, Dr Diana Rose, Patricia Chambers, Dr Julie Ridley. |
|---|---|
| 2 March 2009 | 'What's in a name? Race, user involvement and "hard to reach" communities', Jayasree Kalathil, Survivor Research. 'Effective involvement in mental health services: the role of assertive outreach and the voluntary sector', Rosie Davies, Bristol Mind. 'Politics of recognition: what can a human rights perspective contribute to understanding users' experiences of involvement in mental health services?', Lydia Lewis, Department of Sociology, University of Warwick. |
| 6 April 2009 | 'In-sight–bi-polar self-management', Heather Straughan, Centre for Mental Health Recovery, University of Hertfordshire. 'Not ending with the research report: extending the outcomes into the researched reality', Jasna Russo and Sandra Hamilton, Berlin, Germany. 'Does who we are make a difference to the research that we do? Evaluating the impact of service user involvement in mental health research', Steve Gillard and Kati Turner, Division of Mental Health, St. George's, University of London. |
| 11 May 2009 | 'How personality became treatable', Martyn Pickersgill, Institute for Science and Society, University of Nottingham. 'Women, alcohol and mental health: achieving authenticity in a hostile environment', Patsy Staddon, University of Plymouth. |
| 1 June 2009 | 'A symbolic interactionist approach to mental health outreach', Jim Roe and Hugh Middleton, University of Nottingham. 'Using personal experiences to understand other people's mental health recovery', S. Ajayi, J. Billsborough, T. Bowyer, P. Brown, A. Faulkner, A. Hicks, J. Larsen, P. Mailey, R. Sayers and R. Smith, *Rethink*. Discussion of the seminar series and ways forward. |

## Participant comments

### *What did you enjoy most about these seminars?*

"The opportunity to listen to and discuss presentations of service user and survivor research alongside more directly sociological mental health presentations – also equally the opportunity to get to know the BSA [British Sociological Association] study group members and SRN [Survivor Research Network] community better after the seminars."

"Opportunity to network; finding out about other people's work."

"Fresh approaches and perspectives – quite different from the presentations I am mostly used to."

"Hearing about innovative projects and ideas; networking."

"Being able to listen to other user researchers' research topics/interests and the networking opportunities during these seminars."

"The papers were short, but very good and there was plenty of time for open discussion, which was very engaging."

"It allowed user and professional researchers to learn from each other."

"The friendly exchange of ideas – ideas about the sociological relevance of user research (useful, as I teach sociology)."

"Opportunity to hear and network with assorted people and disciplines and original thinkers."

"The opportunity to be up to date on the research being conducted and the difficulties encountered. The convivial nature of the interaction, particularly in the later seminars."

"Spirited mix of different kinds of perspectives, discourses and debates."

"The opportunity to hear from people working on challenging the status quo with new and fresh ideas, and examples of their work."

"Really, really, really interesting and informative. At the informal bit in the pub later, I had some excellent in-depth discussions that were as enlightening as the seminars."

"Stimulating mix of people. Perspectives that were challenging."

## Further comments and suggestions for future events

"It would be good to have more seminars of this nature as they seem to bridge the gap between service users and mental health workers. Debate on these important issues could really move us forward."

"I think it would be a good idea to continue pairing SRN researchers with BSA Study Group researchers on themed seminars."

"It's important that a sociological focus is retained ... [to ensure] challenges to conventional thinking."

"I thought the idea of further developing a relationship between user groups and the BSA is both timely and full of potential for future activities."

"I would definitely be up for attending future seminars. Thanks for organising them!"

# Index

Note: Page numbers followed by 'n' indicate footnotes.

## W

## Z